ALSO BY CHARLES J. CHAPUT

Strangers in a Strange Land:
Living the Catholic Faith in a Post-Christian World

Living the Catholic Faith: Rediscovering the Basics

Render unto Caesar: Serving the Nation by Living Our
Catholic Beliefs in Political Life

THINGS WORTH
DYING FOR

THINGS WORTH DYING FOR

THOUGHTS
ON A LIFE
WORTH LIVING

Charles J. Chaput, OFM Cap.

Henry Holt and Company   New York

Henry Holt and Company
Publishers since 1866
120 Broadway
New York, NY 10271
www.henryholt.com

Henry Holt ® and ® are registered trademarks of
Macmillan Publishing Group, LLC.

Scripture quotations are from the Revised Standard Version of the
Bible—Second Catholic Edition (Ignatius Edition), copyright © 2006 National
Council of the Churches of Christ in the United States of America. Used by
permission. All rights reserved.
Distributed in Canada by Raincoast Book Distribution Limited

Library of Congress Cataloging-in-Publication Data

Names: Chaput, Charles J., author.
Title: Things worth dying for : thoughts on a life worth living / Charles
J. Chaput, O.F.M. Cap.
Description: First edition. | New York : Henry Holt and Company, 2021. |
Includes bibliographical references.
Identifiers: LCCN 2020034254 (print) | LCCN 2020034255 (ebook) |
ISBN 9781250239785 (hardcover) | ISBN 9781250239778 (ebook)
Subjects: LCSH: Christianity. | Life—Religious aspects—Christianity. |
Christian life—Catholic authors. | Spiritual life—Catholic Church. |
Apologetics. | Catholic Church—Doctrines.
Classification: LCC BR85 .C143 2021 (print) | LCC BR85 (ebook) | DDC
248.4/82—dc23
LC record available at https://lccn.loc.gov/2020034254
LC ebook record available at https://lccn.loc.gov/2020034255

Our books may be purchased in bulk for promotional, educational, or
business use. Please contact your local bookseller or the Macmillan Corporate
and Premium Sales Department at (800) 221-7945, extension 5442, or by
e-mail at MacmillanSpecialMarkets@macmillan.com.

First Edition 2021

Designed by Kelly S. Too

Printed in the United States of America

1 3 5 7 9 10 8 6 4 2

FOR ALL THE SAMS

with gratitude and friendship

"Anyone who has truly known God can never be cured of him."

François Mauriac

CONTENTS

THINGS WORTH
DYING FOR

1

IF I FORGET THEE, O JERUSALEM

"Without memory there is no culture. Without memory there would be no civilization, no society, no future. . . . That is my major preoccupation, memory, the kingdom of memory. I want to protect and enrich that kingdom, glorify that kingdom, and serve it."

Elie Wiesel

AT NIGHT, LOOKING NORTH ALONG THE COAST FROM Jaffa, the Tel Aviv skyline rises out of the sea like a circus of light against a black sky. Termed "the Mediterranean capital of cool" by the *New York Times*, the city is Israel's economic and creative nerve center, a brash sibling to its elder brother, Jerusalem, just forty-five miles up the road.

The average age of Tel Aviv's populace in 2019 was thirty. A flourishing social life fuels five-star restaurants and hotels. Foreign embassies and government offices dot the streets. High rises of steel and glass shape the horizon.

Violent crime is rare. In a region of chronic conflict, the city is remarkably safe. Greater Tel Aviv enjoys one of the highest standards of living in the Middle East.

Its founders would be proud. They built better than they knew.

Tel Aviv-Yafo, the city's full name, began as an empty sand dune and sixty Jewish families. The year was 1909. Tired of the crowding in nearby Jaffa ("Yafo" in Hebrew), the families moved outside the ancient town. They set about creating, from nothing, a modern, self-run Jewish community, the seed of a new Israel. They designed it on a modern urban model. It had proper streets, sanitation, and construction. And their labors took root. Inspired in part by the dream of a revived Jewish nation in the historic Jewish homeland, they committed themselves to building a source of hope for Jews everywhere. After Israel declared independence in 1948, Tel Aviv annexed largely Arab Jaffa in 1950.

The key to Tel Aviv's DNA is its pride in a new Israeli identity. It rejects any captivity to the past. Israel's national Holocaust museum, Yad Vashem, keeps alive the memory of Jewish suffering at the hands of a hostile world, especially in the Shoah. But Tel Aviv is young. It turns itself firmly toward the future.

The trouble with the future, though, is that it's tied inescapably to the past. It grows from our choices and actions here and now. The future gestates in the present, and the present is formed by the past. Jaffa, the womb that birthed Israel's "capital of cool," is vastly older than

Tel Aviv. Humans have lived in the place now known as Jaffa for 3,500 years.

Jonah set sail for Tarshish from Jaffa in his flight from God. Solomon brought cedars from Lebanon through Jaffa's port in building the First Temple. Peter healed Dorcas in Jaffa and had the vision that convinced him to preach to gentiles. Canaanites, Egyptians, Assyrians, Babylonians, Greeks, Romans, Byzantines, Persians, Muslim caliphates, Crusaders, Turks, French, British: All have ruled here. All have disappeared into history. All have added to the weight of the past.

As in Jaffa, so throughout Israel—or Palestine, or the Holy Land; the name itself is a source of friction. It varies according to how one views this small strip of geography at the crossroads of Europe, Asia, and Africa. Trade routes have curved along the coast here for millennia, like arteries feeding the limbs of a body. So too have armies. Sometimes their goal has been wealth; sometimes imperial ambition. But something more precious than gold is in the soil here, especially in Jerusalem. The land is God-haunted, soaked in meaning and often in blood. It is *qadosh*, the Hebrew word for "other than," set apart, sacred. Both Jews and Palestinians see this geography as their home. Both have arguable claims. But their political conflict is compounded by a religious history thick with rival notions of purpose and destiny.

Americans tend to be bad at history. We're a nation founded as a *novus ordo seclorum*, a new order of the ages. Israel is different. In Israel, the past is a living force.

Elie Wiesel, the Nobel laureate, marveled at his people's—the Jewish people's—profound "desire to remember. No other people has such an obsession with memory."[1] For Jews, modern Israel incarnates the biblical Promised Land. Jerusalem is Israel's historic capital and Judaism's sacred city, immortalized in the longing of Psalm 137: *If I forget thee, O Jerusalem, let my right hand wither.* And the Temple Mount is Jerusalem's holiest site. Solomon built the First Temple here nine hundred years before Christ. The Babylonians destroyed it in 587 BC. Rebuilt in 516 BC, the Second Temple was enlarged by Herod the Great in the decades before the birth of Jesus. The Romans leveled it in AD 70, during the First Jewish Revolt. They then destroyed the city and exiled its people during a second revolt some sixty years later.

After AD 70, Jewish religion shifted from temple worship to synagogue. But Jerusalem's Western Wall—the only surviving remnant of the Second Temple—is a site of constant pilgrimage. To this day, at the heart of the Temple Mount lies a rock known as the Foundation Stone. In Jewish tradition, this rock is where heaven and earth meet. It's where God began the creation of the world, and where Abraham tried to sacrifice his son. And therein lies a problem, both political and religious. Because the stone sits under the Dome of the Rock.

Built in AD 691, after the Muslim conquest, the Dome of the Rock is one of Islam's most sacred sites. Like the Jews, Muslims see the Foundation Stone as the place where God set creation in motion. But they also revere it as the spot where Muhammad began his Night Journey to heaven. The Al-Aqsa mosque, also on the Temple Mount, is linked to the same belief. The result of these conflicting claims for the Mount is a chronic state of tension with political implications and no solution.

And then, of course, there are we Christians.

The land now ruled by Israel and the Palestinian Authority includes Bethlehem, where Jesus was born; Nazareth, where he grew to adulthood; and all of the towns and villages where he preached, healed, and taught. In Jerusalem he was circumcised as an infant and visited with his family as a child. It's where he wept over the city, taught in the Temple, and harried the moneychangers. He ate the Last Supper there with his apostles, prayed and suffered arrest in Gethsemane, was judged by Pilate, was scourged and crucified, and died. And in Jerusalem, he rose from the dead.

Every day of the year, pilgrims choke the city. The Christian population has dwindled here and across the Middle East due to war and persecution. But the Holy Land has a uniquely strong pull on the global Christian community. The pull is so strong that it can trigger a peculiar mental state: Jerusalem syndrome.[2] Israeli authorities report about fifty cases each year of visitors who suddenly believe they're King David, or John the Baptist, or Mary about to give birth to the Messiah. These are aberrations. But the yearning to touch the supernatural, the hunger to be in the presence of the eternal, is buried deep in human nature. Thus the holy sites have been a magnet since the earliest days of the Church. The evidence is everywhere:

strewn about the land are reminders of the Holy Land's holy wars—Jewish, Muslim, and finally Christian.

In 1095, Pope Urban II preached the First Crusade. His goals were simple: to aid the Byzantine Empire; to free the Holy Land from Muslim control; and to protect Christian pilgrims, who were often murdered or enslaved. As the great Cambridge historian Jonathan Riley-Smith noted, motives for joining the Crusade were often a mix of Godly and baser appetites. But the main spirit was intensely religious—for the Crusade's leaders and faithful, it was an "armed pilgrimage."[3]

It's hard for many moderns to understand the scope of the Crusade enterprise, the sincerity of its purpose, or the sacrifices required. Men walked, starved, and fought their way for four years across three thousand miles of alien terrain and climate, against great odds, to finally retake Jerusalem, Jaffa, and other cities of the Levant in 1099. Warfare of the time involved fierce brutality on all sides. Suffering on the march was intense. Disease was chronic. Confusion and fear were constant. Many thousands died on the way. Few saw any material gain. Most returned home in poor health and penniless. And all risked their lives, at least in part, for things with no monetary value: the remission of sins, the defense of fellow believers, and a passion for their faith and the honor of God.

Israel, Palestine, the Holy Land: The names differ. The claims differ. They share a present—sometimes glittering, too often painful—that sits atop very different versions of the past. But it's a past oddly uniform in its memories of things worth dying for.

※

IN THE FALL of 2019, just before starting these pages, I turned seventy-five. For bishops in the Catholic Church, that marks retirement age. As canon law requires, I offered my resignation to the Holy Father, Pope Francis.

It was a curious moment. Maybe endings always are. Socrates once said that the unexamined life is not worth living, and memory is the tool for the task. It's the diary of our experiences and their lessons. One of the great blessings in my life was to serve, for a time, as bishop of Rapid City, in South Dakota, then Denver, and finally Philadelphia. Each of those communities is a great city. Each lives in my memory. Stepping down from that kind of life-giving work brings with it feelings of both gratitude and nostalgia.

The good news about turning seventy-five is the time that becomes available for rest and reflection. The not-so-good news is what sooner or later comes after it. By a person's mid-seventies, the road of life in the rearview mirror is a lot longer than the road ahead. A theme like "things worth dying for" takes on some special urgency. As a sardonic friend likes to say, dying is a one-way off-ramp.

Or that's one way of looking at it. My own feelings are rather different.

My dad was a mortician in a small Kansas town. As a

family, we knew and were known by nearly every other family in the community. Many were warm friends. Home was a good place with a lot of happiness. We lived upstairs from the funeral parlor, and for me, that never seemed strange. As I grew older, I would, on occasion, help my father receive the deceased. In our home, death and all of the complex emotions that surround it were a natural part of living. There was nothing dark about it. Death in the community mirrored the cycle of seasons and farming all around us. I learned early, by seeing very intimately, the beauty and sacredness of life, and also its fragility. I learned that mourning is a good thing. It acknowledges that someone unique and unrepeatable has left the world; a life filled with its own universe of joys, sufferings, and loves has passed; a life once linked vividly to so many others is now sustained only in memory.

I also learned, from my parents and many others, that death isn't an end; it's a beginning. God and his mercy are real.

Time has a purpose. The meaning of a sentence becomes clear when we put a period at the end of it. The same applies to life. When we talk about things worth dying for, we're really talking about the things worth living for, the things that give life beauty and meaning. Thinking a little about our mortality puts the world in perspective. It helps us see what matters, and also the foolishness of things that, finally, *don't* matter. Your hearse, as my father might say, won't have a luggage rack.

Thus this book: less a methodical argument or work of

scholarship, more a collection of thoughts on a theme that seems to grow in importance along with the years. There are two great temptations that I've seen people struggle with over my lifetime. The first is to try to create life's meaning for themselves, which translates in the end to no meaning at all. The second is to live and die for the wrong meaning, the wrong cause, the wrong purpose. The world is full of disguised and treasonous little gods that demand our full attention and in the end betray our deepest longings. But there is only one god, the God of Israel. And only in him, as Augustine said 1,600 years ago, can our hearts finally rest. So we begin.

Socrates was one of history's greatest minds. He's often seen as the founder of the Western ethical tradition. He said that his philosophizing was best understood as a preparation for dying. It sounds like an odd claim, but it makes perfect sense. He had a passion for truth telling, for the wisdom that comes from it, and for the life of integrity that results. The very word "philosophy" captures his love for truth. It ties *philia*, the Greek word for "friendship-love," to *sophia*, which means "wisdom." Socrates didn't "study" wisdom. He pursued it as the framework of his life. He *loved* it as a friend.

Love is demanding. It draws us outside ourselves. The more we love, the greater our willingness to sacrifice. When we know, honestly, what we're willing to sacrifice for, even to die for, we can see the true nature of our loves. And that tells us who we really are.

We're surrounded by examples. Families, at their best,

are an exercise in self-denial for those we love. An extreme and heroic example is the Jewish mothers and fathers during the Holocaust who gave their children away to Christian families to save them. They knew the cost of that sacrifice. To offer a more common example: even with the power of modern medicine, every woman who bears a child puts her life on the line. And raising children always requires sacrifices from parents in time, attention, and resources.

Instinct obviously plays a big role in the bond between parent and child. When viewed from the outside, this can make the sacrifices in a family seem "easy." That's because for most people they come naturally. But it's also important to note that as religious belief recedes, and communities of faith decline, the individualism at the heart of modern societies becomes more selfish and corrosive. It breaks down even family bonds. It tempts parents to treat their children as ornaments, or, even worse, as burdens. It also saps the ties between grown children and their parents—who, as they age, can often become dependent, and thus a heavy expense in time and resources.

Another example: Friendship is generally a milder form of love than family, and the notion of dying for a friend might seem remote. But as Jesus himself said, "Greater love has no man than this, that a man lay down his life for his friends" (Jn 15:13). History is full of stories of soldiers who put themselves in harm's way to save their comrades. And all true friendship requires a readiness to die—if not literally, then in the sense of dying to ourselves, dying to our impatience and our reluctance to make sacrifices for others. The willingness to be with our friends when they're not easily lovable, to accompany them in their neediness or to share in their suffering: this is the test of true friendship.

Yet another example is the love of honor. The legends and myths of antiquity often hinge on it. In *The Iliad*, one of history's great epic poems, Achilles withdraws from the Greek army because its leader, Agamemnon, has offended his honor. For centuries men dueled to the death to defend their honor. Women too struggled to prevent their honor from being violated. Protecting one's honor is something that untold thousands have been willing to die for.

"Honor" is a word that can seem theatrical or outdated to the modern ear. But that's simply a defect of our times. Honor is profoundly important. We expect it from others, and we want it for ourselves. It's linked to the idea of dignity or integrity. When a man stays faithful to his wife, he honors his wedding covenant and secures the integrity of his marriage. The same goes for our deepest convictions: they also need to be honored. We all have a hunger—even when we fail at it—to live as honorable people, people of principle willing to speak for what we know to be right and true.

The novels of Aleksandr Solzhenitsyn are filled with people who strive to live honorably in the toxic world of Soviet communism. A gulag survivor himself, his work echoes with disgust for cowards and flunkies, and with reverence for persons who honor their consciences even when doing so risks dying. The settings for his novels are bleak, and today the great murder regimes of the last century are history. Their perils can seem remote. But wickedness, like a virus, has a genius for mutating into new and appealing forms, and Solzhenitsyn's themes are still instructive. Evil is real, even when it's masked by soothing words and excellent marketing. Thus it's always vital to honor our convictions. And doing so usually has a cost.

We live in a time of vindictive political discourse on matters ranging from sex to the meaning of our national history. Our politics often seems gripped with amnesia about the price in human suffering extracted by the bitter social experiments and poisonous Big Ideas of the last century—always in the name of progress and equality.

Obviously our courage needs to be guided by prudence. In the early years of Christianity, the faithful suffered waves of persecution. Church Fathers criticized those who were too eager for martyrdom. The account of St. Polycarp's martyrdom tells us that, at the urging of friends, he initially withdrew from his city to avoid the civic leaders who required Christians to offer sacrifice to pagan gods. Polycarp's discretion is contrasted with the actions of a man who was foolishly eager to defy the authorities as a show of faith. Polycarp, not the rash man, is advanced as the right model of faith.

Life—*all* life, no matter how poor, infirm, unborn, or disabled—is a precious gift. We should never unwisely risk it. The same can be said for professional success, or even just the ordinary good of earning a decent living and providing for a family. Avoiding situations that force us to state our convictions can sometimes be the prudent course of action.

But we need to be careful. The key word in that sentence is "sometimes." Cowardice is very good at hiding behind prudence. Too often we twist ourselves to suit what we think is approved behavior or thought. We muffle our beliefs to avoid being the targets of contempt. Over time, a legitimate exercise of prudence can degrade into a habit that soils the soul. No person of integrity betrays his or her convictions; mouthing lies we know to be lies murders us inwardly. Even silence, which is sometimes prudent, can poison our integrity if it becomes a standard way to avoid the consequences of what we claim to believe. Jesus urges us to love our neighbor as ourselves. Love can never involve accepting or joining in the evil of others. The self-love proper for a Christian includes the love of personal honor, the kind that comes from living with integrity in a world that would have us betray our convictions.

❧

FAMILY, FRIENDS, HONOR, and integrity: these are natural loves. Throughout history, men and women have been willing to live and die for these loves. But as Christians we know that all human loves, like the human instinct for beauty, flow from the Author of love, from the heart of God himself. Thus the highest, purest, *supernatural* love is love for God as our Creator and Jesus Christ as his Son. For this reason, St. Polycarp, for all his caution and prudence, eventually did choose martyrdom rather than compromise his Christian faith.

The issue at hand in these pages is this: Are we really willing to do the same, to follow the example of Polycarp—to be "martyrs" and public witnesses to our faith—and if so, how must we live to prove it? These are serious questions. They're brutally real. Right now Christians in countries around the world are facing the choice of Jesus Christ or death. The German novelist Martin Mosebach published an account of twenty-one migrant workers in Libya who were kidnapped by Muslim extremists in 2015 and beheaded for their faith.[4] Twenty were Coptic Christians from Egypt. One was another African who refused to part from his brothers in the faith.

The murder of those twenty-one men was captured on video. It's hard to watch—not just because the act is barbaric but also because, in our hearts, we fear that, faced with the same choice, we might betray our faith to save our lives. Put bluntly, the martyrs, both ancient and modern, frighten us as much as they inspire us. And maybe this makes perfect sense. Maybe it's a version of the biblical principle that fear of the Lord is the beginning of wisdom. Fear of martyrdom is the start of an honest appraisal of our own spiritual mediocrity.

So we should ponder this fear more deeply, rather than repressing it, as we so often do.

The Christian men beheaded on a Libyan beach are not so remote from us. The worry we naturally feel, that we might fail a similar test, is a concrete version of the anxiety we rightly feel when we think about coming before the judgment of God. If we're honest, we know that we're likely to fail that test too. We're barely able to live up to the basic demands of the Ten Commandments. Many of us have trouble following even the minimal norms of a Catholic life: regular confession and Mass attendance, kindness to others, and a few minutes of daily prayer. If those simple things are struggles, how can we possibly have the courage to face martyrdom? Or the judgment of a just God?

The Christian faith we share doesn't deny or excuse our failures. Sin is serious. It separates us from God and requires conversion. The Church calls us to repentance. But in doing so as a mother, she wants us to see that our hope lies not in our own strength but in the unrelenting fidelity of God's love. As St. Paul says in one of Scripture's most moving passages, "I am sure that neither death, nor life, nor angels, nor principalities, nor things present, nor things to come, nor powers, nor height, nor depth, nor anything else in all creation will be able to separate us from the love of God in Christ Jesus our Lord" (Rom 8:38–39).

What I've learned looking back on my life is that all of us, in all of our strengths and weaknesses, are powerless to defeat God's purpose in Jesus Christ. Our flaws, our mistakes, our mediocrity, even our most ingenious acts of self-sabotage—all are impotent to part us from God's love, *if we turn to him with an open and humble heart.* For this reason, the martyrs do *not* bear witness to their own moral strength as remarkable men and women. They point instead to the relentless love God has for each of us in Jesus Christ. As the Preface for Holy Martyrs reads:

> For you [God] are glorified when your saints are praised;
> their very sufferings are but wonders of your might:
> In your mercy you give ardor to their faith,
> to their endurance you grant firm resolve,
> and in their struggle the victory is yours,
> through Christ our Lord.

What that means is this: those who are faithful to God will in turn have his faithfulness at life's ending, no matter how extreme the test.

Grace illuminates nature. The supernatural love of God in Jesus Christ that gives courage to the martyrs helps us to better understand the natural loves of family, friends, honor, and integrity. The power of these loves—a power so great that we can live and die to remain true to them—doesn't come from within. A mother doesn't conjure love for her child out of her inner emotional resources. The same holds true for friends, honor, and integrity. Love's power draws us *out* of ourselves. It comes from what is loved, not the one who loves. Created in the image of God, the unborn child is *worthy* of a mother's love. It's the worthiness of what we love, its lovability, that enables us to sacrifice time, comfort, wealth, success, and even our lives.

Those of us in the so-called developed nations, even

in the midst of our many challenges, live in an era of stunning wealth. For many of us, the entire globe is open to travel. To a degree unimaginable in earlier ages, many of us can choose our own path in life or even reinvent our identity. As a culture, we seem to float in a fluid world of limitless choice. This can seem like a blessing, but it often turns out to be a curse. That's because only a life without weight, without substance, can float.

The most telling feature of our era is that it weakens bonds. It curves us in upon ourselves. It seduces us to live without love. We're smothered in sweet-sounding slogans like "Love wins" and "Hate has no home here." But so often these words are merely masks for resentment, weapons in a culture war filled with more poison than honesty. We're promised celebrity on social media; escape through our products, technologies, and travel; and riches by virtue of professional success. But we're not really allowed to love. Authentic love turns us away from ourselves and toward the Other. It's ordered to truth: the truth about human beings, human nature, and Creation. It's demanding and self-denying. It anchors us to realities that are deeply human, deeply rewarding, and the deepest sources of joy—but also inconvenient and easily seen as burdens.

It's a good thing, a vital thing, to ask what we're willing to die for. *What do we love more than life?* To even pose that question is an act of rebellion against a loveless age. And to answer it with conviction is to become a revolutionary; the kind of loving revolutionary who—with God's help—will someday redeem a late-modern West that can no longer imagine anything worth dying for, and thus, in the long run, anything worth living for.

❧

AN ARCHAEOLOGIST ONCE quipped that digging in the soil of the Holy Land is as delicate as brain surgery. It can enrich our understanding of the past, and therefore of ourselves. It can also threaten both. The memory of a religion or a people, like the memory of a person, gives shape and purpose to life. The Holy Land is filled with sites revered by three great religions and central to their identities. Some sites have pious tradition for support. Others have hard evidence.

Over the millennia, the original site of King David's biblical capital was lost as Jerusalem grew, was destroyed, and grew again. In the late nineteenth century, excavations to search for it began on a ridge just south of the Temple Mount. The location was an Arab neighborhood in East Jerusalem now known as Wadi Hilweh. After Israel took control of East Jerusalem in the Six-Day War, archaeological digs sharply increased. And with them, so did tensions between Arabs and Jews. Today Wadi Hilweh shares its soil uneasily with Israel's City of David National Park. The site is a treasure trove of Jewish history and a global tourist attraction. Its ancient ruins and artifacts are stunning.

Even more striking is the work underground. The great Pilgrimage Road that linked the Pool of Siloam, where

Jewish pilgrims ritually purified themselves, with Herod's Second Temple was discovered, cleared, and restored. The importance of the find can't be overstated. This was the main thoroughfare of Jewish worship in Roman times, six hundred meters long and eight meters wide. Jesus walked this road, both as a child and as a man. So did his family. So did his disciples and friends. But these wonderful discoveries also pose a problem. The City of David's priceless excavations damage the equally precious Arab homes above them. And many Arab families see the project as a threat to their own long religious roots and an effort to "Judaize" their community.

In a skeptical age, the "Holy" Land can seem like an icon of unholiness—with religion the villain at its root.

The late British scholar and skeptic J. H. Plumb, like many in his discipline, argued that the historian's purpose is "to see things [in the past] as they really were."[5] Much of the past, he believed, is framed in fabricated storytelling. Real history is thus "basically destructive." Celebrated and influential in his time (he died in 2001), Plumb had little use for grand narratives or the claims of any religion. He saw all past systems of belief as mythologies used to justify power and dominate others. For Plumb, history should be liberated from inherited prejudices. It should destroy illusions. As a tool of social science, it should weaken the imagined past with the hard reality of facts, undermining the stories told by earlier generations to interpret the purpose of life in historical terms.

History, he claimed, "is not the past." Rather:

> The past is always a created ideology with a purpose, designed to control individuals, or motivate societies, or inspire classes. Nothing has been so corruptly used as concepts of the past. The future of history and historians is to cleanse the story of mankind from those deceiving visons of a purposeful past [that have so often been used for] the subjection and exploitation of men and women, to torture them with fears, or to stifle them with a sense of their own hopelessness. The past has only served the few; perhaps history may serve the multitude.

And yet, despite his views, Plumb had a grudging respect for the legacy of Jews and Christians. These particular believers "gave a new significance to life." They trusted in an unfolding human destiny. They worked a revolution in human thought and culture "more dramatic, more far-reaching, more absolute, than that experienced by any other great civilization." Plumb feared that many of his own secular colleagues, in contrast, had taken refuge in the meaninglessness of history. He saw that destroying the coherence of the past could cause a paralysis in social matters. He knew that humans "need a compulsive sense of the value of man's past," not only for themselves as persons but also for the world at large.

In the end, Plumb's distaste for what he called the "old past" was largely a dislike for the Christian content that filled so much of it with purpose and shaped it so deeply. In its place, he hoped history would "step into its shoes, help to sustain man's confidence in his destiny, and create for us a new past as true, as exact, as we can make it, that will help us achieve our identity not as Americans or Russians, Chinese or Britons, black or white, rich or poor, but as men."

On the question of how a "basically destructive" tool might build that new destiny, Plumb remained silent.

Which brings us to another, more immediate question: What do all these words about memory and the past have to do with you and me? As a historian, Plumb granted, reluctantly, that "the Christian myth dies hard." He saw that as a problem, as irritating rubble on the road to a better future. But in reality, the "Christian myth" dies hard for a reason.

Like Plumb, C. S. Lewis in his atheist days felt that all religions were essentially myths about who we are and why we're here. For Lewis, all myths were lies—at their best, beautiful lies "breathed through silver."[6] It was his friend and fellow scholar J. R. R. Tolkien who showed him that truth exists whether we like it or not, that truth is always more than a bare collection of facts, that myths can sometimes be true, and that one very particular myth actually happened and was Truth incarnate.

Jesus of Nazareth really did live. He was a man in history, a man of flesh and blood, not a legend but vastly more than one. He preached and taught and healed in the land we call "holy," just as the Gospels say he did. He really was the *Christos*, the Anointed One, the Messiah. He really did suffer and die and rise for us. And the proof is the fire he left in the hearts of those who knew him, a passion that reworked the course of the world. When he took Jerusalem's Pilgrimage Road for the last time, riding a donkey and cheered by a mob, Jesus knew the malice, betrayal, and crucifixion that awaited him. He knew that some in the same mob would very soon call for his death. Many others would see no meaning in his sacrifice. And yet he still gave his life for us, out of love for us. In the mind of Jesus, we—despite ourselves, despite our failures, despite the confused creatures we so often are—were worth dying for.

And since that's so, and if we mean what we say when we call ourselves Christians, surely we can at least *try* to live and die for others.

If I forget thee, O Jerusalem, let my right hand wither. The French mystic Simone Weil once said that "the destruction of the past is perhaps the greatest of all crimes."[7] Along with all of its achievements, the world we've built ensnares us today in a permanent present, a narcotic cocoon of distractions and appetites, here and now. It erases our past. It makes us forget. *It steals the memory of who we are as Christians and why we're in the world.*

St. Paul tells us that "God did not give us a spirit of timidity but a spirit of power and love and self-control. Do not be ashamed then of testifying to our Lord . . . but take your share of suffering for the Gospel in the power of God" (2 Tim 1:7–8). As Christians, we have a future because we have a purpose and a destiny beyond ourselves, a mission passed down to us to renew the face of the earth with God's love through the Gospel of Jesus Christ. We need to reclaim those gifts—each of us in our own lives as individuals, and together as a Church. And this means that as believers we can expect a difficult road in the years ahead on a whole range of issues. There can be no concordat between the Christian understanding of human identity, dignity, and sexuality and the contempt directed at our beliefs by so much of our emerging culture. The world and its hatreds won't allow it.

The structure of the pages ahead is simple.

Chapter 2 speaks to how we should think about death and the verdict it passes on the lives we live. Chapter 3 examines the culture we have now—a culture of irony soured into cynicism, a culture of deriding and refusing the questions that death raises, and the desert of meaning that results. Chapter 4 is about the Author of our lives, the true God and our source of meaning, and our chronic temptation to evade him. Chapters 5 through 8 examine the things—sometimes ennobling, sometimes idolatrous—that so many of us consider worth living for and dying for: nation, ideas and ideologies, family and loved ones, and the Church herself. Chapter 9 speaks to the nature of our earthly pilgrimage and the "four last things" we each inevitably face. And an afterword reflects on friendship: friendship with God and friendship with each other—the essence of Christian life, and a foretaste of the life to come.

My thoughts these days often turn to the author and scholar J. R. R. Tolkien. The drama of the Christian story shaped everything Tolkien wrote; the intensity of his Catholic faith grounded his entire life and genius. Near the end of *The Two Towers*, the second volume of Tolkien's great Lord of the Rings trilogy, Samwise Gamgee says, "The great tales never end, do they, Mr. Frodo?" And Frodo answers, "No, they never end as tales, but the people in them come and go as their part's ended."[8]

At seventy-five, my part in the tale is ending. But the Church, her mission, and the Christian story we all share: these go on. And so the greatest blessing I can wish for those who might one day read these words is that you take up your part in the tale with all the energy and fire in your hearts. Because it's a life worth living.

GENTLE, INTO THAT GOOD NIGHT

"And he will guide them to springs of living water; and God will wipe away every tear from their eyes."

Revelation 7:17

IT'S ONE THING TO TALK BRAVELY ABOUT "THINGS WORTH dying for." But as the 2020 coronavirus showed with brutal clarity, it's quite another to think seriously about what dying involves, why we need to die at all, and what if anything comes after the moment that we all eventually face: our own death.

The poet Dylan Thomas, who himself died young, spoke for the human species when he penned the lines, *Do not go gentle into that good night / Old age should burn and rave at close of day; / Rage, rage against the dying of the light.* Death is humanity's great mystery. Nobody of sound mind and in decent health wants to die. And yet we must.

My friends who are doctors and nurses deal with the

deaths of their patients in different and curious ways. Some turn to God, others to dark humor. Many grow an emotional shell. It's understandable: They're trained to restore health and extend life. But in the end, life is finite. Even when they succeed, they merely push the inevitable a little further down the road. The endgame is always, and often palpably, in the background of their efforts.

Priests are even more acquainted with death. We're free of the burden to heal bodies, but the emotional weight of reaching out to souls gripped in the end by fear or anger, regret or bitterness, can be just as heavy. We counsel the dying, listen to and forgive their sins, bury the dead, and comfort surviving family and friends. We do it, moreover, as one of the central tasks of our vocation. In half a century of priesthood, I've celebrated hundreds of funerals and burials. Without prayer, even something as sacred as consigning a person to God can become, for the priest, a routine drained of meaning—until it strikes close to the heart. The familiarity of routine is no vaccine against sorrow when death comes for persons near to the priest himself. In the decades since my ordination, I've been present for four deaths. One was that of my closest friend. Another was my mother's. Both were moments of beauty. And both were intense experiences of loss.

In death's shadow, the idea that we own our own bodies and selves and command the course of our lives is, as the devil Screwtape would say, "equally funny in heaven and in hell."[1] So a little sober thought about the unthinkable is in order.

Human beings are, by nature, "subcreators." It's the word Tolkien used to describe how people take part in God's creative power. What we build, or "subcreate," expresses our concerns. For many centuries, man's grandest buildings were tombs and temples. A civilization's main concern was honoring its gods or its dead, or both. Athens revered the goddess Athena, and so the greatest edifice we find in Athens is the Parthenon. The same principle held in Christian cultures. Aside from a royal palace, a city's greatest building was usually its patronal church or cathedral, the palace of Christ the King and the sanctuary of his mother and the saints.

Cities honored the dead in a similar way. The Vatican's Scavi tour passes through an underground Roman cemetery, down an ancient street of tombs. In effect, the Roman elite built a city of the dead that mirrored the world of the living. Great pagan rulers built huge tombs as homes for the afterlife and to glorify themselves in the eyes of their descendants. Egypt's pyramids are monuments of a culture obsessed with death. Egyptian royals commissioned lengthy books with incantations to protect the dead from demons. They filled their tombs with food and treasure, even burying slaves alive, to prepare their entry into the life to come.

Cities today are different. We can build higher, faster, and more lavishly than any civilization before us. But the signature buildings and public spaces in New York or Shanghai have a different purpose. Our temples of glass and steel are full of stores, office space, and elegant restaurants. Our focus isn't divinity. Nor is it our dead ancestors. Our primary concerns are work and play, getting more money and spending it. We avoid dwelling on death, or the afterlife, or the dead themselves. We prefer to ignore them.

Comparing our public monuments that commemorate the dead tells the story. London's Cenotaph memorial, built a century ago, honors those who died fighting in the bloodbath of World War I. It's a tall, austere coffin hewn from stone, decorated with a wreath. It rises toward the sky, a somber acknowledgment of the dead, and it calls us, the living, to remembrance and reflection. In contrast, New York's 9/11 Memorial is two square waterfalls occupying the space where the World Trade towers once stood. Their water disappears into a black square whose depth we cannot see. The Cenotaph points to something above. The 9/11 Memorial, for all its solemn, striking beauty, hints at the deep ambiguity of the grave.

The Cenotaph and memorials of antiquity have meanings rooted in religious belief or honor codes of the past. Today, as we noted earlier, the word "honor" and its duties can taste like dust on the tongue. We flee the constraints of tradition. We make our own meaning. We create our own significance—or we try to. Many people choose to have their ashes strewn in a place which they alone find meaningful; they simply scatter into the carbon of an uninterested world. They leave no trace or memorial of their loves, their joys and sorrows, or their lives. Thus it's hardly a surprise that in 2019, Washington State legalized human composting as a green alternative to burial and cremation. And to help the process along, a company called Recompose hopes to speed up the natural course of body decomposition. "We know a lot about the process," CEO Katrina Spade said, "because we're not so different from livestock really, but it had never been proven with humans."[2]

In a sense, of course, this is true: humans decompose like other mammals. But trends like human composting suggest that our efforts at making our own meaning have taken an odd turn. Again, this shouldn't surprise us. As Pope Benedict XVI once observed:

> Meaning is the bread on which man, in the intrinsically human part of his being, subsists. . . . But meaning is not derived from knowledge. To try to manufacture it in this way, that is, out of the provable knowledge of what can be made, would resemble Baron Munchhausen's absurd attempt to pull himself up out of the bog by his own hair. . . . Meaning that is self-made is, in the last analysis, no meaning. Meaning—that is, the ground on which our existence as a totality can stand and live—cannot be made but only received.[3]

The churches and tombs of the past marked how we know who we are, and they pointed to a transcendent source of our moral compass. They were symbols of the faith and inherited wisdom that bound us, the authorities to which we owed obedience and love. Refusing those sources of meaning only quickens our flight from facing the reality of death. Death exposes the emptiness of our work at self-made meaning. In the end, erasing ourselves from the memory of others has a curious kind of logic if our lives really have no purpose, if we're just a more advanced form of cattle.

Hans Jonas was a Jewish philosopher who searched for the good and true after the tragedy of Auschwitz. He noted that humans have three artifacts that set them apart from all other animals: the tool, the image, and the grave. No other species buries or remembers its dead as we do. The grave is a uniquely human fact; it reminds us that we're not like other animals. Thus, repudiating the grave implicitly denies our distinctive humanity by denying one of its most important markers.

The grave also underscores two other human qualities. First, as Jonas said, "among all beings, man is the only one who knows that he must die." Cows and cats may fear danger, but they don't know that they will die. Second, while we know we must die, we also hope to defy mortality. Our graves point to an unseen and immaterial purpose, to something that declares that death will not have the final word. Our graves show that man is an animal of thought and spirit who "raises his thinking to the realm of the invisible." In the words of Jonas, "Metaphysics arises from graves."[4]

Knowledge of death may be uniquely human. But death marks all living creatures. Life depends on the world around it and its contingencies. It can end, and often does, due to factors beyond our control. "Life, in other words, carries death within itself," Jonas observes. "Being has become a task rather than a given state, a possibility ever to be realized anew in opposition to its ever-present contrary, not-being, which inevitably will engulf it in the end."[5]

We all fear the fading of youth and the approach of death. We also know that we can't escape them. How a culture deals with death reveals how it thinks about the meaning of life and the nature of the human person. We humans die, but in dying we transcend the cage of the material world and its clock. Death touches every life with a sense of tragedy but also the chance for nobility. Denying it, refusing to face it, or draining it of its meaning steals something profoundly human from life.

🌿

THE PROSPECT OF losing life is bitter, but also moving. It can sharpen our awareness of beauty and intensify our loves. There are good reasons to fear death: the pain of possible suffering, the loss of loves and friendships, the finality of our own insignificance, and the plausibility that nothing at all comes next. All of this seems to undermine any meaning to life. But for those who believe, Jesus Christ has made death into the gateway to eternal life with God. The Resurrection clarifies the meaning of life, and therefore the meaning of death. It teaches us that appropriate fear, ruled by appropriate hope, is the nature of a good life. The path to death should be one of trust and abandonment.

Scripture has much to say about death. Genesis begins with the creation of the world as an overflowing of God's goodness. According to various Christian theologians, death was a natural part of the world even before the Fall, at least for lower forms of life.[6] But before the arrival of sin, man and woman ruled peacefully over creation and lived in communion with God and one another. God commanded that they might eat of every tree in the garden except for the tree of the knowledge of good and evil, "for in the day that you eat of it you shall die" (Gen 2:17).

We know the rest of the story. Adam and Eve ate of the tree at the urging of the serpent. Their eyes were opened to their nakedness. Their desire to be like God led to a rupture in their relationship with him, between themselves, and with the rest of creation. And while they did not die immediately, God declared that they would return to the earth out of which they were formed: "[For] you are dust, and to dust you shall return" (Gen 3:19).

On the one hand, death is simply the punishment for humanity's sin. Genesis sees death as an evil, alien to human nature and not part of God's intended plan. Originally, our soul and body worked in harmony with God's will. When we chose to sin, our wills became disordered; this disorder was mirrored in our bodies, leading to corruption and decay.[7] On the other hand, God can take human disobedience and use it to bring about new, good things.

That becomes clear in Christ's resurrection. But many who lived before Jesus's time had a different view. In the

Old Testament, death was seen as the natural human end, but never as a blessing or something good.[8] The Israelites hoped for a long, distinguished life, a life with comforts and many children to carry on the family name and bury the deceased. A premature death, without children or a proper burial, was a dreadful fate. But even a long and rich life was lived in death's cold shadow. As the book of Ecclesiastes says, "If a man begets a hundred children, and lives many years; so that the days of his years are many, but he does not enjoy life's good things, and also has no burial, I say that an untimely birth [i.e., a stillborn child] is better off than he" (Eccles 6:3). Death was a grim inevitability.

In the Psalms too we see how the early Jews viewed death and the way it shaped their relationship with God. They believed that the dead were consigned to Sheol, or "the Pit," a place of shadow. God's power was present in Sheol, but the dead had no intimate relationship with him.

The Psalmists are clear that the dead in Sheol are not living in divine light. Their lot is something much less than life on earth. When the Psalmist is in peril, he cries out: "For my soul is full of troubles, and my life draws near to Sheol. I am reckoned among those who go down to the Pit; I am a man who has no strength, like one forsaken among the dead, like the slain that lie in the grave, like those whom you remember no more, for they are cut off from your hand. You have put me in the depths of the Pit, in the regions dark and deep" (Ps 88:3–6).

Most tellingly, the dead don't perform the greatest of all human activities: *worship*. They do not praise God. Psalm 115 makes this clear: "The dead do not praise the Lord, nor do any that go down into silence" (115:17). Psalm 6 does the same: "Turn, O Lord, save my life; deliver me for the sake of your merciful love. For in death there is no remembrance of you; in Sheol who can give you praise?" (6:4–5).

The Old Testament is filled with appeals against death based on this same premise: God should save me from death, so that I can praise him *in this life*. The prophet Isaiah writes that God has held back his life from the pit of destruction because "Sheol cannot thank you, death cannot praise you; those who go down to the Pit cannot hope for your faithfulness. The living, the living, he thanks you, as I do this day" (Is 38:18–19). And the Psalmist cries out: "To you, O Lord, I cried, and to the Lord I made supplication: 'What profit is there in my death, if I go down to the Pit? Will the dust praise you? Will it tell of your faithfulness? Hear, O Lord, and be gracious to me! O Lord, be my helper!'" (Ps 30:8–10).

The Psalms, for all their beauty, are a bracing tonic. Without the hope of resurrection, death offers no comfort, even for those who love God.

The book of Ecclesiastes, probably written during the time of the Persian Empire, has similar themes. This was a period of great economic activity fueled by the introduction of standard money. Money became a commodity, something people desired for its own sake. More people had more access to wealth, but at greater economic risk. A volatile economy led to insecurity. People worked hard to get ahead, but they also knew the fragility of their world. Ecclesiastes is a reflection on our futile attempts to control life in the face of uncertainty—especially the greatest uncertainty, death.[9]

For the author of Ecclesiastes, everything is vanity. Life is a chasing after the wind. Death is inevitable: "Everything before them [the righteous and wise] is vanity, since one fate comes to all, to the righteous and the wicked, to the good and the evil, to the clean and the unclean, to him who sacrifices and him who does not sacrifice. As is the good man, so is the sinner; and he who swears is as he who shuns an oath. This is an evil in all that is done under the sun, that one fate comes to all" (Eccles 9:1–3).

Enjoy your life now, the author urges; eat bread and drink wine: "Enjoy life with the wife whom you love, all the days of your vain life which [God] has given you under the sun, because that is your portion in life and in your toil at which you toil under the sun. Whatever your hand finds to do, do it with your might; for there is no work or thought or knowledge or wisdom in Sheol, to which you are going" (Eccles 9:9–10). Given the hardness of its words, Ecclesiastes can easily sound like an invitation to despair. But dismissing it would be a mistake. We need to read Scripture canonically, each book as part of the whole, unfolding Word of God, each book illuminated by the others. Ecclesiastes shows us what earthly striving looks like without the hope of resurrection.

※

OF COURSE, DEATH and Sheol are not the only story that the Old Testament tells. As Harvard scholars Kevin J. Madigan and Jon D. Levenson observe, a tension exists between two competing theological ideas in the Old Testament. One idea sees Sheol as the last stop for all men and women. It's a notion that fits well with the pagan cultures surrounding ancient Israel, cultures that saw human destiny as one of dominant gloom. The other idea contrasts those who go to Sheol with others who die blessed, like Abraham, Moses, and Job.[10]

Indeed, the Old Testament speaks of God swallowing up death forever (Is 25:8) and raising up people from Sheol (1 Sam 2:6). The prophet Isaiah says that the dead do not live, but then he writes: "Your dead shall live; their bodies shall rise. O dwellers in the dust, awake and sing for joy! For your dew is a dew of light, and on the land of the shades you will let it fall" (Is 26:19). And the book of Daniel speaks of the dead awakening, "some to everlasting life, and some to shame and everlasting contempt. And those who are wise shall shine like the brightness of the firmament, and those who turn many to righteousness, like the stars forever and ever" (Dan 12:2–3).

This is the opposite of what we find in Ecclesiastes, where the wise and wicked alike share the same end. So what's going on? As Madigan and Levenson powerfully suggest, we can see in the Old Testament how Israel comes to understand, more and more deeply, what it means that God is victorious over death:

> What has happened with the biblical Sheol, it seems to us, is that the affirmation of faith in the omnipotent and rescuing God of Israel, against whom not even the most formidable of enemies can ultimately stand, has collided with the brute fact of death, with all the negative denotations that death generally had in Mesopotamia and Canaan. Something had to give. What gave was not the faith in the limitless power of the Rock of Israel and their redeemer. What gave was death.[11]

If Israel's early view was that all men end up in Sheol, a different view emerges in the quoted passage from Daniel. A final judgment will take place. The good person will be rewarded and the wicked punished. This belief was held by many by the time of Jesus's birth.

Throughout his ministry, Jesus healed the sick. This was a sign of his mercy and his role as Messiah. But it was also a symbol of resurrection. For us, a sharp break exists between life and death. Many ancient Israelites thought that the break existed, instead, between a healthy, successful life and a life marked by hardships. Today we see the sick as a subset of the living. The Israelites often saw them as a subset of the dead. Per Madigan and Levenson: "The Psalmists [saw] illness as continuous with death and thought of the reversal of illness as so miraculous as to be in the nature of a return to life, an exodus from Sheol."[12] Jesus's healing miracles are thus "mini-resurrections," fore-tastes of the ultimate power he will exercise over life and death.

We see that power when Jesus raises Lazarus from the dead. This story is famous for many reasons, among them the shortest verse in the Bible: "Jesus wept" (Jn 11:35). At first glance, this weeping seems to make no sense. Jesus loved Mary, Martha, and Lazarus, but he quite deliber-ately chose to wait two days before going to the tomb. He knew that Lazarus was dead. Yet he delayed, because he would use his friend's death as an occasion to show his power over the tomb and decay. Death is still, none-theless, the main tragedy of the human condition, and Jesus shows us the proper response before it: deep sor-row. God became man, and when he confronted death, he wept.

Jesus's confrontation with death grows as he approaches his own crucifixion. Sorrow is compounded with trepida-tion as he prays in the Garden of Gethsemane. "My soul is very sorrowful, even to death," he told his disciples (Mt 26:38). The Gospel of Matthew has Christ twice pray that the suffering he's about to undergo might pass from him, "nevertheless, not as I will, but as you will" (Mt 26:39). In the Gospel of John, Jesus says, "Now is my soul troubled. And what shall I say? 'Father, save me from this hour'? No, for this reason I have come to this hour. Father, glo-rify your name" (Jn 12:27–28).

Benedict XVI notes that this passage from the Gospel

of John goes beyond the sorrow that Jesus felt at the death of Lazarus. He writes: "In this way John is clearly indicating the primordial fear of created nature in the face of imminent death, and yet there is more: the particular horror felt by him who is Life itself before the abyss of the full power of destruction, evil, and enmity with God that is now unleashed upon him, that he now takes directly upon himself, or rather into himself, to the point that he is 'made to be sin' (cf. 2 Cor 5:21)."[13]

The death of Jesus is the moment when Life itself enters into death. Then it emerges victorious. Traditional Resurrection icons show Jesus not bursting forth from an empty tomb but "descending into hell," in the words of the Apostles' Creed—into the realm of death, into Sheol. Jesus has ripped the doors off the hinges and pulls Adam and Eve out of their prison. The ground is littered with keys and shattered locks in the background. This is nothing like the raising of Lazarus. It's something altogether new.

As Benedict puts it:

Jesus' resurrection was about breaking out into an entirely new form of love, into a life that is no longer subject to the law of dying and becoming, but lies beyond it—a life that opens up a new dimension of human existence. Therefore the resurrection of Jesus is not an isolated event that we could set aside as something limited to the past. . . . [Rather,] a new possibility of human existence is attained that affects everyone and that opens up a future, a new kind of future, for mankind.[14]

The early Christian community marveled over what this new future entailed. The truth was, and is, simple but radical. Those who have been baptized into Jesus Christ, who are now part of his body, share in his death and resurrection. Jesus has "abolished death and brought life and immortality to light through the gospel" (2 Tim 1:10). Christ is now the Lord of the living and the dead (Rom 14:9), who holds the keys to death and Hades (Rev 1:18).

St. Paul was perhaps the greatest expositor of the Resurrection's meaning. He gives us the enduring tension in Christian faith regarding death. At the end of time, death will be crushed completely when Christ puts all his enemies under his feet: "The last enemy to be destroyed is death" (1 Cor 15:26). Death remains an evil and our enemy, a bitter source of sorrow and lamentation. And yet, because we share in Christ's resurrection, death is now the door through which we pass to a more intimate union with God. Thus Paul can also say that "For me, to live is Christ and to die is gain." To depart this life and to be with Christ is a blessing (Phil 1:21–23).

≫

ANCIENT CIVILIZATIONS AND today's secular societies, as we've seen, offer us two extremes in responding to death. Ancient societies understood death and ritualized it, sometimes brutally, as part of a rhythm of Creation mandated by the gods. Loss and suffering were bitter. They couldn't be avoided. But they belonged to a heavenly design shared by and governing all, a design that was ultimately, in some sense, satisfying.

Modern societies are very different. In their liberal form, they're mute on any transcendent meaning to life. Thus they're silent about the meaning of death, beyond a nod to the grieving and an admission that it's sad. They do this in the name of respecting the diversity of individual beliefs. But the effect is to undermine the bonds of community by diminishing the gravity of a universally shared and intense experience. It thus cripples any shared sense of purpose that might rightly require a person to sacrifice in society's service.

The root of that word "sacrifice" is telling. It derives from the Latin words *sacrum facere*—to make sacred; to set aside as holy. A culture that dismisses (or worse, derides) the holy and ignores the sacred has very little license to ask any sacrifice from anyone.

The Bible is clear that death is an evil. Without the prospect of God's redemption, death is a source of terror and a temptation to despair. In Gerard Manley Hopkins's phrase, "It is the greatest of earthly evils. It robs us of our all."[15] But in the resurrection of Jesus, death has new meaning. Our Christian faith reminds us that we die like other animals, but we're also much more than other animals. It teaches us to erect and reverence graves. It tells us to remember, mourn, and pray for the dead. It counsels us to be mindful of our own deaths—in Latin, *memento mori*; roughly, "remember you must die"—and to live our lives in light of their end. But it also gives us hope for life beyond the grave.

The *memento mori* tradition has a long history in Christian thought. But it's useful first to see it in context.

Long before the birth of Jesus, many philosophers had already seen that the pagan myths about gods and goddesses were false. So were popular nightmares about death. The Roman scholar and statesman Cicero, in his *Tusculan Disputations*, argued that death is not an evil. Terrors of the underworld are fictions, he wrote. There are two possible outcomes in death. If the soul is immortal, as most human cultures seemed to hold and most philosophers believed, then death is a deliverance from the burdens of the material world. But if the soul is merely mortal, then it dies with the body. There can be no suffering in an afterlife that doesn't exist. This would make death not a horror but, rather, the moment when we're finally freed from evil altogether.[16]

Since death delivers us, Cicero stressed, we shouldn't fear it. We might even long for it:

> For if [our] final day brings not annihilation but a change of place, what more can be wished for? But if, on the other hand, [it] brings total destruction and obliteration, what can be better than to fall asleep in the midst of the toils of life and so, closing one's eyes, be lulled into everlasting slumber? . . . [If death] seems a sentence delivered by God that we depart from life,

let us obey joyfully and thankfully and consider that
we are being set free from prison and loosed from our
chains, in order that we may pass on our way to the
eternal home which is clearly ours, or else be free of all
sensation and trouble.[17]

This kind of thinking, though it sounds mild, is unhap-
pily cold comfort.[18] It makes death the end of something
bad, not the dawn of something good. Death may loosen
our chains. But the reality and nature of an afterlife are, at
best, ambiguous.

The Gospel offers us vastly more. Christians believe
that death is not just the end of pain but the beginning
of an endless joy, not just the loosening of burdens but a
new start of endless intimacy with a loving God. Compare Cicero's words to these from Dom Philippe Dupont,
abbot of the Abbey of Solesmes, in France: "In a monastery, we do not cry for the dead. That must not be seen as
a lack of feeling on our part. We know where our brothers
are going. The burials [of our brother monks] are always
joyful. Our existence must be a novitiate for eternity. The
entire liturgical life of a monk prepares him for the final
hours."[19]

Cicero argued eloquently about death but claimed
no certainty about an afterlife. The monks of Solesmes
meet death with the confidence of faith. Their hope in
the Resurrection is not just positive thinking or clever
self-delusion. It's an unshakable rock on which they can
stand, in good times, yes, but even more so in the midst

of suffering. Their lives are an ongoing preparation for death.

The journalist Nicolas Diat visited the great monasteries of France, including Solesmes, to talk with monks about death in their communities. Diat observed that, for the monks, death isn't just an event we undergo; it's a path to walk and help others to walk. Too often today, many of us do not know how to die. The sacred sense of passage our culture once attached to death no longer exists, but our fear and anxiety have never been stronger.[20] The monks whom Diat spoke with know how to die.

Diat tells the story of one Brother Vincent, a young monk at Lagrasse Abbey, who died of multiple sclerosis. "The more he advanced toward God, the less his brothers understood him," Diat writes. "He had become transparent."[21] The hardship of the man's suffering moved the community deeply. It became a heavy cross for him and his brothers to bear. Nevertheless, Brother Vincent met death in a spirit of abandonment. "I gave everything to Jesus," he said. "He has taken everything. I thank him."[22]

Diat notes that when a monk like Brother Vincent suffers too much, he can no longer sustain the effort of prayer as he once did: "In these moments, a mysterious alchemy is created; the patient is picked up by the flow of the prayers of the other monks. The man who is going to die can no longer row the boat, but he goes forward with his brothers."[23]

When death approaches, monks are there to help and encourage a dying brother. But death isn't something alien to them. They prepare for it every day of their shared religious life. Brother Philippe, the infirmarian at Cîteaux, told Diat that thinking properly about death is far from morbid. Rather, it enables us to understand the meaning of life: "Real life is not on earth. Every day, we must prepare to die."[24] Dom Innocent, a Carthusian monk at the Grande Chartreuse monastery, observed that we are born to meet God and that monks desire this most of all: "A monk has given his life to God, and he has never met him. It is normal for him to be impatient to see him."[25] This impatience allows many monks to meet death with peace. They're not eager for death itself but for what lies beyond it. That requires mature faith and hope, nourished over time with prayer and practice. These allow the soul to rest confidently in God's love, even at the end of life.

A prayer to Mary, the mother of Jesus and our mother, by Father Jérôme, a monk of the Abbey of Our Lady of Sept-Fons, captures this hope-filled faith beautifully:

During my life you have held me by the hand, O my Mother. Could it be that at this hour I feel your fingers loosen and your hand let go of me? Certainly not! If your sovereign hand were leaving my hand, it would undoubtedly be to take a fold of your mantle and cover me with it, Mother of my long journey and Mother at my ultimate moment, yes, wrap me in the fall of your mantle during this short moment, after which, sure of having passed through the gate, I will suddenly let go, to make you hear my laughter. The laughter of a child, who laughs, who laughs, because, with the help of his Mother, he has achieved all.[26]

This kind of trust and abandonment is the great hallmark of the Christian response to death. Yes, death is a sorrow and an evil. Jesus wept before it, and so can we. But Jesus also overcame it. By faith in him, we can live out our lives in the shadow of death, knowing that a dawn follows, striving to use well the time God has given us, and hungry for union with him in heaven. As the American priest and public intellectual Richard John Neuhaus said at the end of his life, "The entirety of our prayer is 'Your will be done'—not as a note of resignation but of desire beyond expression."[27]

3

THE WATERS OF CASABLANCA

"Irony is just honesty with the volume cranked up."

George Saunders

WRITING AMID THE COUNTRYWIDE TURMOIL THAT FOLlowed the May 2020 racially charged killing of George Floyd by Minneapolis police, a columnist noted the hatreds and hopelessness of America's "new nihilism" and claimed that "this is not 1968. It's worse."[1] Given the fierce social divisions that marked the civil rights and Vietnam era—years I remember vividly, while I studied for the priesthood—it was a tall claim. But not a foolish one. I would only add that our nihilism is not new. It's been ripening for decades, and for reasons that warrant some thought. We're not the nation we once were.

I grew up in flyover country, otherwise known as Kansas. Concordia, my hometown, sits on the southern side of the Republican River in the Smoky Hills region of the Great

Plains. North central Kansas is a very long way from the coasts, and not merely in miles. This is farm country. It always has been. The land is green and fertile. The air is clean. Life takes place on a human scale.

In 1944, the year I was born, the town had a newspaper and about 6,500 souls, the largest concentration of people and their stories for many miles around. Camp Concordia, just north of town, still held about 4,000 German prisoners of war, mostly from the fighting in Africa. Life in the camp was easy. Escape attempts were few; there was, after all, no place to go. The prisoners worked on Concordia's outlying farms, and relations with locals were generally good. Friendships were made that lasted for decades after the war. It was that kind of world, a world where the pronoun "we" had more weight than "I."

We were an ordinary family. I don't remember which of my parents had a bigger role in shaping my beliefs as a child. Both my mother and my father were strong examples of Catholic faith. As I look back on them, I'm astonished at how much they knew about the faith and how well they knew their catechism, even though neither had a university education. My mother trained as a nurse, but she didn't have a college degree. My father trained as a mortician and embalmer, and he had certificates for that from embalming school, but nothing more.

Religion was central to our family, and not merely as a set of rules. It was the anchor of the life we shared. My father came from a family of fourteen. Two of his siblings were Sisters of St. Joseph. My mother came from a family of eight. Both of her parents died before she was fifteen years old. She was sent to a boarding school, and then she was on her own. We had good relationships with her family, and with my father's. Concordia had a heavy French and Canadian Catholic presence. We went to Mass together every Sunday and confession together every two weeks. We prayed the rosary almost daily when I was very young. And my parents sent all of us—I'm one of three children—to the town's Catholic school.

The thing I remember most about home was my father kneeling at his bed every morning and every evening, and my mother praying her devotionals every day with the prayer book she carried along with her rosary. Faith was a regular part of our routine. Like the land and the seasons, there was nothing artificial about it. On a summer Kansas evening, alone with a sky like the vault of heaven, and stars whose beauty seemed to cancel gravity, a child's imagination could run free. The sacramental, the supernatural, the wondrous and mysterious: for me, these were intimately real.

From my parents I learned how to love. They also taught me the difference between right and wrong, and that we're in the world not as critics or spectators but as main actors in the greatest of stories. Like it or not, we *matter*, and so do our actions. What we do or don't do has consequences—in this world and beyond it. As a result, the notion that a human being, with all of his or her irreplaceable emotions and thoughts, is simply a mix of chemicals that finally runs out of energy has always struck me as implausible, a disguised form of resentment for the messiness and seriousness of life.

We thirst for something more. The dignity of our intellects and our connections with other people, the love we freely give and receive, and the experiences of God that so many of us have: all these things point to a meaning beyond this world. They teach us that human beings are immortal in a very real, personal, and particular way, and not just as a matter of family memory or poetic imagination or being absorbed somehow back into the universe. Whatever the outcome of our journey here on earth might be, each of us is forever.

Flyover country, it turns out, had the space and the quiet for such thinking. My parents filled both with the food and water of the mind: books. As a child, I'd wander off, again and again, into the world of a book. My mother would struggle to get my attention. The imagination of other people, their skill at creating entire worlds different from my own, took part in some mysterious way in God's own authorship, and the stories always absorbed me—which is why I also loved movies, all kinds of movies, from a very early age.

I've seen hundreds of films, some of them two or three times. For me the best films, like the best novels, hinge on the characters, their choices under pressure or in the heat of conflict, and the consequences that follow. Choices always have a cost. In choosing one course of action, we close off all other courses, sometimes at great expense. How characters handle those choices and costs is the stuff of drama. It's also the stuff of life. My own favorite movies tend toward stories like *A Man for All Seasons*, *The Exorcist*, and *The*

Silence of the Lambs. But most people, being laypeople, are either married, or want someday to be married, or at least hope at some point to meet a romantic soulmate. So they have a special taste for love stories. And very few love stories in film come close to the power of *Casablanca.*

Made in 1942, amid the Second World War, *Casablanca* is, to quote too many reviewers to count, "the greatest Hollywood movie of all time." Set in Casablanca, in Vichy France–controlled Morocco, it's the story of Rick Blaine (Humphrey Bogart). Once an idealist and a daring gun smuggler for antifascist freedom fighters, Rick is now a burned-out cynic nursing a secret wound. He runs an upscale nightclub for stranded foreign refugees while verbally fencing, in a friendly way, with the charming and hypocritical chief of police, Captain Louis Renault (Claude Rains). Into the nightclub one evening walks Ilsa Lund (Ingrid Bergman). Ilsa is the woman Rick once passionately loved; the woman who left him abruptly, without explanation, for a husband (played by Paul Henreid) she'd never told him about. The husband character, Viktor Laszlo, is a famous resistance leader. He and Ilsa are on the run from the Nazis; they need Rick's help to flee Casablanca. The rest is movie history.

Filmmakers often describe their work as a "cathedral art." Like a medieval cathedral, a film is only as good as its many different craftsmen: writers, producer, director, cameramen, editor, actors, set designer, and others. Any one of them can ruin the product. This is what makes the near perfection of *Casablanca* so miraculous.

Making the film was a chaos of ambiguities, imperfections, and above all, ironies.[2] Neither Bogart nor Bergman was a big star. Their on-set chemistry was cordial, but not close. Bogart was short and had to stand on a box for romantic scenes with his costar. The writers were rarely more than a day or two ahead of the shooting schedule. And the writers themselves didn't know how to end the story until the last few days of the production. The iconic final scene between Bogart and Rains—"Louis, I think this is the beginning of a beautiful friendship"—was shot as an afterthought, weeks after the production wrapped.

From Rick's claim in an early scene that "I stick my neck out for nobody" to Captain Renault's "Major Strasser has been shot; round up the usual suspects" near the close, the story is veined throughout with irony. And nowhere is the irony more delicious than here:

> Renault: *"What in heaven's name brought you to Casablanca?"*
> Rick: *"My health. I came to Casablanca for the waters."*
> Renault: *"The waters? What waters? We're in the desert."*
> Rick: *"I was misinformed."*

Irony, as the author George Saunders once suggested, is just honesty with the volume cranked up.

❧

IRONY IS A double-edged sword. It's a powerful tool, and also a lethal weapon, in every language. It can be elegant and dry (as employed by Rick Blaine above). It can be horrifying (Heinrich Himmler, the Third Reich's mass murderer, wept at the beauty of Schiller's poetry). It can amuse (*The Red Army Choir Sings Christmas* might bring a smile, and yes, it's a real recording). It can enlighten, humble, and instruct. It's the Swiss Army knife of a talented wordsmith.

Irony has its roots in ancient Greek comedy. It comes from the word *eironea*, meaning pretended ignorance or dissimulation. Irony has many definitions and applications, but they all boil down to a gulf between what is said or expected and the reality that actually is. This resonates with the experiences most people have in everyday life—which is why, at its best, it can be such a great teacher. Anyone can understand and learn from irony, even when it wounds, because it doesn't require an audience of geniuses. All it demands is a bit of common sense, a little self-knowledge, and the willingness to put some critical distance between ourselves and our own presumed importance. Irony captures the incongruities of being alive. And, in that sense, it is indeed honesty with the volume cranked up.

So no one should be surprised that the Word of God is thick with irony.

Consider: the God who creates the stars; sets the planets in motion; fashions humanity out of dirt; drowns Pharaoh's chariots; thunders on Sinai; and commands the rejection of all other gods—this same God listens patiently to a nomad named Abraham who, step by step, like a haggler in a Casablanca bazaar, wheedles him down in a deal to save the innocents of Sodom and Gomorrah. This is a God who is all just but all merciful, fiercely demanding but infinitely forgiving, chronically faithful to the chronically faithless.

Very few lines in all of Scripture pack more irony than God's laconic answer to the querulous and suffering Job (38:4): "Where were you when I laid the foundation of the earth?" And in the New Testament, the transcendent Maker of all things becomes one of us. God chooses a Galilean teenager for the mother of his son and a Bethlehem stable for Jesus's birth. The human body itself, the world of flesh redeemed at bitter cost by Christ's physical death and resurrection, is simultaneously intricate, beautiful, wondrously made, hilariously awkward, embarrassing, and weak. The God of the Bible has a sense of humor and an exquisite taste for irony, along with all of his commands to be righteous—including the impossible (in this world) call to be perfect as he is perfect.

At its best, argued the philosopher Roger Scruton, irony is one of the two pillars of the civilization we call "the West." The other pillar is forgiveness. We inherit both from our Jewish and Christian roots. The ironic temperament

> [is the] habit of acknowledging the otherness of everything, including oneself. However convinced you are of the rightness of your actions and the truth of your views, look on them as the actions and the views

of someone else and rephrase them accordingly. So defined, irony is quite distinct from sarcasm: It is a mode of acceptance rather than a mode of rejection. It also points both ways: Through irony, I learn to accept both the other on whom I turn my gaze, and also myself, the one who is gazing. . . . Irony is not free from judgment: It simply recognizes that the one who judges is also judged, and judged by himself.[3]

This understanding of irony and the humility it can engender has public and political, as well as profoundly personal, consequences:

The West's democratic inheritance stems, I would argue, from the habit of forgiveness. To forgive the other is to grant him, in your heart, the freedom to be. It is therefore to acknowledge the individual as sovereign over his life and free to do both right and wrong. A society that makes permanent room for forgiveness therefore tends automatically in a democratic direction, since it is a society in which the voice of the other is heard in all decisions that affect him. Irony—recognition and acceptance of otherness—amplifies this democratic tendency and also helps thwart the mediocrity and conformity that are the downsides of a democratic culture.[4]

Note that while Scruton (d. 2020) had great respect for religious traditions, especially Judaism and Christianity, his own views about God could be ambiguous. There's a caution in that for us. Personal witness, not merely intellectual assent, is key to a life of faith. Part of that witness involves a willingness to examine ourselves honestly and repent of our own many sins. The roots of our culture are largely biblical, and they dry up very quickly without the water of a lived and self-scrutinizing Christian faith. Still, Scruton did see clearly that happiness "does not come from the pursuit of pleasure, nor is it guaranteed by freedom. It comes from sacrifice. . . . And in the Judeo-Christian tradition, the primary act of sacrifice is forgiveness. The one who forgives sacrifices resentment, and thereby renounces something that had been dear to his heart."[5]

All true, and all urgently needed today in a nation of pent-up frustrations and grievances. Mercy is a central lesson of the Gospel. So is forgiveness. But then what happens to justice?

The difficult fact about pursuing justice is this: it's vital to a humane and well-ordered society; it's the cornerstone of all credible law; and yet it can rarely be fully achieved. The tangle of humans' interlocking wounds, fears, poisoned memories, and debts is too old and too vast for anyone to unravel. But *enough* justice—even if imperfect—can be had when it's leavened with a measure of mercy, the free act of forgiving, and the letting go of some debts that we know others owe to us. Letting go allows others to do the same. It heals and gives peace. It breaks up and washes away the toxic ice of resentment that chokes the heart. And in doing so, it takes on a Godly irony that gives life.

※

UNFORTUNATELY, FEW THINGS are more tempting to the palate than the taste of humiliating one's enemies and desecrating the things they hold dear. "Deconstructing" other people's beliefs in the good, the true, and the beautiful, while claiming our own righteousness or intellectual superiority, is a delicious exercise in power. To complete our humanity we need to unlearn the appetite for it. We do that by training ourselves in the habits of patience, generosity, and magnanimity. But we no longer have a culture that does this.

Liberal society is good at many things. Instilling moral coherence, and a shared sense of things worth living and dying for, is not one of them. As "I" has displaced "we" as the favored pronoun of Americans, opportunities for conflict have multiplied and abscessed—with the result that for the modern cynic, as much as for the modern ideologue, contempt for the interior peace and convictions of others is the emotional equivalent of crack cocaine.

A sign of the calculated hatred in some of the street demonstrations of 2020 was the damage done to churches, churches that had long been active in the work *against* racism. Racial injustice is one of America's original sins. Much of the anger that spilled out after George Floyd's killing was legitimate. But like a parasite attaching itself to a healthy body, political hatreds fed on the chaos. Along with public

institutions, history, and monuments, religion itself became
a target of rage against authority. And this made a dark kind
of sense. As religious practice wanes, and faith becomes
little more than a collection of pieties or a tepid habit, its
seeming hypocrisy grows, and along with it, antireligious
contempt.

A common example: Picture a cartoon (taken from the
Internet) of a galaxy in deep space, vastly magnified, with
a sign pointing to a speck of dirt on its tail-shaped rim.
The sign reads "GOD'S FAVORITE PLANET." The
words are simple, and the meaning is clear: *Here's what
those religious simpletons believe in—a Superfairy who cares
about the pathetic concerns of intelligent microbes on a pin-
point of dust in an ocean of complexity.* Only a fool could
be so ignorant.

The point of the cartoon isn't to *disprove* religion but to
make it contemptible. As Saul Alinsky might say, the best
way to crush an opponent isn't to argue with him ratio-
nally, which is much too tedious and dangerous, but to
humiliate him personally. Contempt is a strong toxin. And
sarcasm—weaponized irony—is a great delivery system.

It's worth noting that, aside from its cynical feroc-
ity, there's little new in today's "new" atheism. Its DNA
tracks back three centuries to Voltaire and the French
philosophes. The historian Brad Gregory, among others,
has shown that the latest variant offers nothing original.
Modern atheists claiming the mantle of science fail "to see
how their alleged refutations of the reality of God depend
on their assumptions about what they think theology is.

Posturing as educated intellectuals standing up for critical rationality against naïve credulity, in fact they demonstrate at length how little they know about intellectual matters directly relevant to their concerns."[6]

In other words, the god that atheists debunk is not the God that Christians worship. The unbeliever thinks too crudely but also with overfed confidence. My point here is this: the habit of sarcasm entrenched for decades in our mass media and popular entertainment has now borne fruit in our political culture, and this fuels a deeper illness, a social infection of contempt. In spreading, it creates a nihilist spirit that dissolves community and sets people against each other, exhausting both institutions and individuals.

Part of becoming a mature adult involves developing a healthy skepticism. We have brains for a reason. Anyone who believes everything he or she finds on Twitter, reads in a newspaper, or hears in a television newscast is asking for an ugly surprise. A critical spirit, properly applied, always has value. But a good skepticism is always moderated by humility, hope, and prudence. Cynicism is a very different creature.

Much of today's educated opinion, consciously or otherwise, derives from a secular creation myth. The myth runs on certain assumptions; these include the claims that science, free political institutions, and respect for human rights all flow from the eighteenth century's overthrow of tradition and religious authority. In the place of superstition, the story goes, the Enlightenment brought the light of human reason and the end of magical thinking. It's an elegant myth, convenient and self-affirming for postreligious minds. But at least two problems cripple it. First, as the Israeli philosopher Yoram Hazony has shown, the myth is vastly overstated and in some ways simply false.[7] And second, it's now eating itself.

Hazony notes that "Enlightenment philosophy didn't achieve a fraction of the good [its proponents] claim, and it has done much harm." Its "astonishing arrogance" led to the ruin of institutions like marriage and the family, and a drastic misreading of the nature of human reason.

With perverse irony, "the principal figures of Enlightenment philosophy weren't skeptics. Just the opposite. Their aim was to create their own system of universal, certain truths, and in that pursuit they were as rigid as the most dogmatic medievals."[8] Robespierre, Lenin, Stalin, Hitler, Mao, and Pol Pot—these and other children of the Enlightenment murdered or enabled the murder of tens of millions of innocent victims in the name of "science" or "progress" or "history," a cannibalism fueled by idolatrous ideas.

Debunking Enlightenment vanity has been done before and very well—with little effect on its disciples. We needn't waste time on that work here. But its results are still with us in the cynicism that comes from cratered political dreams and failed social experiments.

Freeing the libido was supposed to make sexual activity more frequent, more fun, and less emotionally tangled. It's done the opposite. As of 2019, American young people were having less sex than previous generations at the same age; they were also having far higher rates of STDs like syphilis.[9] And pornography is now pervasive. Worse, in the words of philosopher Byung-Chul Han, our consumer economy now "aggravate[s] the pornographication of society by making everything a commodity and putting it on display. Knowing no other use for sexuality, it profanes Eros—into porn."[10]

The American marriage rate has declined to a record low.[11] Divorce and domestic turmoil have increased. Sexual identity and gender ideology have morphed from biology into the endless ambiguities of personal choice and pronoun wars.

Free enterprise was supposed to spread democracy around the world. Instead, American tech companies have propped up a repressive Chinese surveillance state.[12] Automation was supposed to ease the life of the American worker. Instead, factories now often demand "white-collar degrees for blue-collar work."[13] Diversity and multiculturalism were supposed to enrich the substance of higher education. Instead, they've often led to ideological extremism and intellectual intimidation.[14]

Globalist efforts toward unity, abstracted and remote from local realities, have fueled nationalism and populist revolt. "Abstraction is the enemy," wrote the essayist Wendell Berry,

> wherever it is found. The abstractions of sustainability
> can ruin the world just as surely as the abstractions

of industrial economics. Local life may be as much
endangered by those who would "save the planet" as
by those who would "conquer the world." For "saving
the planet" calls for abstract purposes and central powers
that cannot know—and thus will destroy—the integrity
of local nature and local community.[15]

The ability to think in abstractions, of course, is a jewel
of human intellect. But like everything else, when distorted, it becomes a curse. The tendency to push toward
an abstract and utopian future, ignoring the lessons of
the past, is a legacy of Enlightenment overconfidence.
Another such legacy is social science. And it's precisely in
the social sciences—which apply the tools of science to
persons as objects—where reason starts to eat itself.

As medical science explores the human brain, it raises
questions about the reliability of human reason. Meanwhile social science—in the name of reason, ironically—
"seeks to convince us that we must entirely stop reasoning
about any notion of a truth beyond the facts." In this way,
argues the scholar Yuval Levin, "it stifles both the freedom
of thought and the search for truth alike, since the two are
inexorably linked."[16]

In other words, reason becomes a weapon against
itself—and us.

Humans have a habit of making the same mistakes again
and again, in new forms, with new costs and excuses. We
do it in each new generation. Our vanity in the present
makes us blind to lessons of the past. It also ensures that

we make the same blunders in the future. The only reliable brake on this cycle of stupidity and pride is a culture's moral character. And that character depends on a shared belief in the goodness, the sacred quality, of something or someone greater than human reason, worthy enough to live and die for. When that's lost, things unravel. And as we're now learning, the results of that unraveling can get ugly.

⚜

IT'S HARD TO imagine a greater irony than dying of thirst on the surface of an ocean. A healthy person can survive two or three weeks without food. Water is a different matter. Without it, the body shuts down in three or four days. The ocean, for a thirsty man, might as well be a desert— only worse. There's water, water everywhere, but not a drop to drink. Ingesting salt water forces the body to pass more water than it takes in, simply to flush out the salt. It makes thirst more, not less, intense. Anyone who's seen films like *Lifeboat* or *Seven Waves Away,* or read stories of William Bligh's struggle to survive on the open sea with loyal crew members after the mutiny on the *Bounty,* can almost taste the unique suffering of slow dehydration on a carpet of liquid that stretches to the horizon.

Many of us, whether we admit it or not, now experience life like survivors of a sunken ship, adrift in a lifeboat, carried along by currents we neither control nor fully understand. The developed world, and we who live in it, float on an ocean of options and anesthetics. But we thirst. Our cleverness, our wealth, and our distractions can't satisfy the deeper thirst that dries up and deadens our souls. Our economy gives us more choices than ever, but the wrong choices for our real needs. For the individual, the result is a spirit of teased restlessness, confusion, resentment, and more anxiety, not less. And our problems don't stay in the first world. We export them globally as elements of the "good life" everyone should desire.

But what exactly is a "good" life? What makes it worthy? For Aristotle, who had such a great impact on Thomas Aquinas, the very idea of the "good life" made no sense without an overarching human nature and the reality of objective human goods. Without such certainties, it's impossible to distinguish the truly good for us from what merely seems so. The good life, the life that brings real happiness, consists in conforming ourselves to our nature and realizing its inherent potential. It's not enough to get what we desire; we must learn to desire well. We do that by cultivating excellence in moral virtue and judgment, in our intellects, and in our unique skills.

Cicero likewise held that personal happiness flows from the discipline of moral virtue. For the happiness of the broader community, he felt that the civic virtues of prudence, justice, fortitude, and temperance were vital. Augustine, reflecting on Cicero, saw that the only "perfect" happiness is the kind of happiness that can't be lost; thus, what we really thirst for is eternal life. To Cicero's list of civic virtues, Augustine added the need for the theological virtues of faith, hope, and charity. The heart is always restless, he wrote in his *Confessions*, until it rests in God. For only God can heal the divided heart forever.

These views contrast sharply with the ideals of our current culture, which presents the good life as a matter of self-invention and acquisition: amassing products and services, fulfilling dreams and appetites. For those who are written off as the weak and the lonely, the failures and the losers, the secular world offers therapies (and medication) when the strain of living gets too burdensome to bear. But while such medical tools can often be useful, reliance on them as a substitute for the more difficult work of living is a cheat on two levels. The first is social. The second is personal.

The Dominican priest and scholar Herbert McCabe observed that

> Society, says the conventional wisdom, exists to protect us from each other; to keep the peace between people with quite divergent views of the good life. This is the theoretical foundation or credo of the secular or liberal society: Society is a peaceful coexistence of potential or real enemies. Friendship and love do not come within the purview of society as such.[17]

There's no "we," only "I"—in other words, no solidarity—when your neighbor might secretly be a foe. But this is the logic of a world with no common, higher bond or meaning. McCabe warned that today's conventional wisdom only makes sense if, despite all our pieties about human dignity, our *real* view of the human person is that of a competitive animal whose actions can be largely explained by neuroscience and evolutionary psychology.

The human "kind," though, is different in kind, not merely degree, from other animals. We humans formulate intentions and goals for ourselves. We have self-consciousness. We have creative capacities. We have autobiographies. Dogs and dolphins don't. These things mark our apartness from the world of objects and other animals. We're more than creatures reducible to a biological category.

As Roger Scruton noted, "the world as we live it, is not the world as science explains it, any more than the smile of the Mona Lisa is a smear of pigments on a canvas. But this lived world is as real as the Mona Lisa's smile."[18] Sincere religious faith, and the contemplation of beauty in classical philosophy, great art, literature, and music: these things remind us of who we are and what we must live up to in our humanity.

Take these things away—ignore them, diminish them, or show them contempt—and we "deprive ordinary people of the ways in which they can represent their apartness. Human nature, once something to live up to, becomes something to live down to instead. Biological reductionism nurtures this 'living down,' which is why people so readily fall for it. It makes cynicism respectable and degeneracy chic. It abolishes our kind, and with it our kindness."[19]

Questions about God, meaning, and human destiny: these, science can't answer. Or it views them as naïve or irrelevant. But they're *precisely* the most urgent questions, the ones that *make* us human and reflect our thirst for meaning. No amount of worldly success or distraction can make them go away. It can only dull their urgency.

Dismissing such questions, and the longings that inspire them, as purely private concerns belittles the thirst for "something more" that we all feel. It steals our joy. It sharpens our loneliness. It worsens our fear of insignificance. It cuts the heart out of community by reducing society to an aggregate of competing appetites, moderated by government and managed by experts. In the end, it fuels an inner restlessness that both stimulates and exhausts. This leads first to frustration and anger, and then to acedia, the lethal fatigue of soul that saps hope and comes as much from frantic activity as from indolence. And acedia ripens finally into despair.

Suicide rates have increased in every US state in recent years, especially among males and the elderly. In the period 1999–2016, twenty-five states saw suicides increase by more than 30 percent, with the Midwest hardest hit.[20] Prescription fill rates for anxiety and depression drugs have also steadily increased—again, with the biggest spikes occurring in places like my home state of Kansas.[21] These problems stem from a range of causes. Easy explanations can be misleading. But in the Midwest, at least one of the triggers is clear: Young people flee rural areas as economic changes destroy traditional farm life. Agrarian culture erodes. And as it does, so do family health and hope in the future.

Anxiety about the future takes different forms for

different reasons around the country. But it runs beneath all of life today like a tectonic fault. Man doesn't live by bread alone—nor by any of the goods, services, therapies, pharmaceuticals, and materialist answers offered to us by the world we've remade in our own image. Nor does a knowing cynicism about the "real" world, irony's toxic mutation, make our thirst for meaning any easier to bear.

Casablanca's Rick Blaine at least has the memory of a lost idealism. His life has substance: he risked it for things he believed in. The chronic posture of contempt toward religion, tradition, and "bourgeois" life so common today in the academy, the political-activism industry, and popular culture is unearned and fatuous. And it's conducted from the comfort of the wealthiest nation on the planet.

A concluding anecdote:

Israel's yearly rainfall has declined since its founding in 1948, and much of its land even then was arid. But while its population and economy have grown sharply, and societies typically waste more water as they grow more successful, Israel has done the opposite. Inventing new irrigation techniques and using them scrupulously, its people have brought large portions of desert back to cultivation and made dead soil bloom with new life. Water did that. Water is life.

In the same spirit, Psalm 63 speaks to us from across the millennia:

> O God, you are my God, I seek you,
> my soul thirsts for you;

my flesh faints for you
as in a dry and weary land where no water is.
So I have looked upon you in the sanctuary,
beholding your power and glory.
Because your merciful love is better than life,
my lips will praise you.

It's thus that John writes in Revelation 22: that the "river of the water of life, bright as crystal, flow[s] from the throne of God," nourishing the tree of life, rich in fruit and with its leaves meant "for the healing of the nations."

Water is life. Water is to parched land as God's Word is to parched souls—the souls of men and women and the soul of a thirsting world. The lesson here is simple. In each of us lives a shadow of the Samaritan woman (Jn 4:1–26) who came to draw water from a well. She found the Source of living water instead. That same living water is extended to us. As Jesus says (Jn 7:37–38), "If anyone thirst, let him come to me and drink."

And from those who *do* drink "shall flow rivers of living waters," waters to renew the world.

FIREMEN AT THE BURNING BUSH

"Everywhere in the world nowadays, the proudest and most ambitious buildings in the center of cities are towers. And at their tops are giant signs that everyone can read with the names of the new gods . . . the mighty of this world."

Jean-Marie Lustiger

AS CATHOLICS, WE BELIEVE THAT AROUND US ALWAYS IS A cloud of witnesses. When we worship at Mass, we're never alone; an unseen family is with us as well. When we sing "Holy, Holy, Holy," we join a chorus of angels and blessed men and women who've gone before us. They lived and died faithfully for God. We honor them for their example of virtue.

A sincere faith leads us to give ourselves to God. But the prospect of handing over our will to a God we can't see, for something so abstract as "eternal life," can seem odd and frightening. Any reasonable person will ask whether theological arguments and invisible realities warrant a life of costly discipleship or even a painful death. Why should we live and be willing to die for God? Why should we love him and want to spend eternity with him? And why should the hope of heaven exhilarate us rather than put us to sleep?

Dante's *Divine Comedy* is a genius work of literature. So is Milton's *Paradise Lost*. But angels and demons are implausible to many moderns. In an age of materialism—which assumes that the physical world is all that exists—the *Comedy*'s structure and inhabitants, and even the sins it describes, can seem absurd. We're tempted to dismiss the idea of "God" as a byproduct of our evolution that we no longer need.[1] And yet, as we've seen, most of us still have a thirst for something more than this life and this world can offer.

What, then, should we do with that desire?

For an answer, we need to ponder who or what the "true God" might be. We need to understand what makes the God of Abraham, who revealed himself most fully in Jesus Christ, unique, worthy of our worship—and even lovable. For Jews and Christians, that story starts with an invasion of human reality from the "outside," with a breaking in of the transcendent. It begins with the light and heat of a bush that burns but isn't consumed, something impossible and yet powerfully real at the same time. It continues with God's revelation on Mount Sinai and his gift of the law to Moses, followed promptly by humanity's first and most common obscenity: the sin of idolatry. The Israelites can't accept who God is, nor who he calls them to be. So they craft a false god, a calf of dead metal, who more conveniently fits their desires and interests.

⸙

THE BOOK OF Genesis is a beautiful story. But it also seeks to show that the God of Israel is the true God, utterly unlike any other gods of surrounding peoples. In some creation myths, a heavenly being is killed and cut open. The world pours forth from the corpse. Others teach that the world is born from the sexual union of gods, or the world was made by a demon or a lesser god. Against these myths, Genesis says that the true God is one god and the *only* god. He has, and will abide, no competitors.

When God first appears in Scripture, we see him as a celestial monarch. He creates the universe, the world, and all its living things. Like a king issuing decrees, God says, "Let it be this way," and it is so. God fashions the world from nothing and then declares it "good." Thus our existence is not a mistake or an accident. It was *intended*. In like manner, Genesis depicts the sun and moon not as other godlike beings—which they were for most other ancient peoples—but as lights that God made to demarcate day from night.

God is described as a ruler in majesty, but also a lover in intimacy. After they eat the fruit of the tree of the knowledge of good and evil, Adam and Eve hear "the sound of the Lord God walking in the garden in the cool of the day" (Gen 3:8). It's an image powerful in its simplicity, redolent of the intimacy of friends resting in each other's presence. That's the kind of closeness Genesis implies we were meant to share with God. There's a sense in which God sought to walk with us and rest with us in a loving communion.

Adam and Eve sin, and God expels them from the garden. But he never abandons them. In the rest of Genesis, especially in the story of Abraham, God reveals himself to be "a Father who keeps his promises."[2] God chooses a particular man. He makes a covenant with him, not only for the benefit of Abraham's family but, through them, for the benefit of the whole world. These chosen people prove themselves imperfect and unworthy. Their election is much more a matter of God's mysterious mercy than their own merit or achievement. We see this in the story of Joseph, whom God uses to save not only the people of Israel but Egypt as well.

However, Egypt forgets this. A Pharaoh arises who "knew not Joseph" (Ex 1:8). He oppresses the Israelites living in Egypt. They cry out to God for deliverance. So God remembers his promises and comes in glory and might to destroy the Egyptians through the help of a powerful and capable general . . . or that's how the story *might have* gone, if you or I had written it. But we didn't, and it doesn't.

Instead, God reveals himself to a fugitive with a speech impediment hiding in the desert as a shepherd. Exodus 3:1–6 recounts the story:

> Now Moses was keeping the flock of his father-in-law, Jethro, the priest of Midian; and he led his flock to the

west side of the wilderness, and came to Horeb, the mountain of God. And the angel of the Lord appeared to him in a flame of fire out of the midst of a bush; and he looked, and lo, the bush was burning, yet it was not consumed. And Moses said, "I will turn aside and see this great sight, why the bush is not burnt." When the Lord saw that he turned aside to see, God called to him out of the bush, "Moses, Moses!" And he said, "Here am I." Then he said, "Do not come near; put off your shoes from your feet, for the place on which you are standing is holy ground." And he said, "I am the God of your father, the God of Abraham, the God of Isaac, and the God of Jacob." And Moses hid his face, for he was afraid to look at God.

The burning bush is one of the Old Testament's two great "theophanies," or self-revelations of God. Most scholars think Mount Horeb is another name for Mount Sinai, where the other great theophany, the giving of the Law, takes place. Both times that God appears on this mountain, he appears as fire, a fire that burns but doesn't consume. There's a paradox in this. God appears in order to reveal himself, to make a more personal union with his people. But he reveals himself in a concealing, inaccessible form. God's taking the form of fire underscores that he is neither tame nor a projection of our desires. God is not material, but, like fire, he is powerful, dangerous, illuminating, and purifying.[3]

In the burning bush, God names himself to Moses.

First, he identifies himself by the covenant he made with the Jewish patriarchs: he is the God of the tribe of Abraham, Isaac, and Jacob. But Moses presses him further. He asks what he should tell the Israelites when they ask for the name of this God that will save them from Egyptian slavery. God then replies: "'I am who I am.' And he said, 'Say this to the people of Israel, "I am has sent me to you."'" God also said to Moses, 'Say this to the sons of Israel, "The Lord, the God of your fathers, the God of Abraham, the God of Isaac, and the God of Jacob, has sent me to you": This is my name forever, and thus I am to be remembered throughout all generations'" (Ex 3:14–15).

Moses seems to expect God to reveal his name so that he can be identified and differentiated from other gods. If you knew the name of a god—so the ancient world reasoned—you could try to manipulate him.[4] But God's name is not a knowable noun. He remains outside man's control. He's not just another local godling in the well-populated pantheon of Middle Eastern deities. The name God gives is not a noun but a verb. And it's grammatically ambiguous. It could mean "I am who I am," or "I will be who I will be."

In a sense, God's name itself invites a relationship. Commenting on these verses, the great French Catholic philosopher and Sorbonne scholar Rémi Brague writes that when the question "Who are you?" is genuine and deep, "when it corresponds to a desire to know the person as such, the only true response is 'You will see.' . . . Moreover, it cannot be given except in an experience rooted in love or friendship. Love consists precisely in the space that is opened, in which the other person can say, or rather, show, what he or she is. Or rather: what he or she *will be*."[5] God is saying that he will show Israel who he is by his actions; in effect, he tells Moses, "You will see."

As promised, God leads Moses and the Israelites out of Egypt and back to Sinai, the earlier site of the burning bush. This time, God gives the people the Ten Commandments and the prescriptions for worshiping him alone. In giving them the law, he shows them the way of right relationship with each other and with God. And God appears as he did in the burning bush—but this time on a far grander scale: "Now the appearance of the glory of the Lord was like a devouring fire on the top of the mountain in the sight of the sons of Israel" (Ex 24:17).

Toward the end of the Sinai story, we read that "the Lord used to speak to Moses, face to face, as a man speaks to his friend" (Ex 33:11). This seems profoundly perplexing, even impossible, since God is wholly "Other." We think of the face as something uniquely human and personal. But for Pope Benedict XVI, the fact that God himself has a "face" means that he's not captured by a static image, to be worshiped as something created by human hands. Rather, God must be related to as a person.[6]

Benedict writes that "Seeking the face of God is an attitude that embraces all of life; in order for a man to see God's face at last, he must himself be entirely illuminated by God."[7] This becomes clear finally in the person of Jesus, who *shows* us what it looks like for a human life to be entirely illuminated by God. Reading God's revelation at Sinai through the lens of Christ's life, and following the Church Father Gregory of Nyssa, Benedict explains:

> [We] can only encounter God by walking after Jesus; [the] only way we can see him is by following Jesus, which means walking behind him and thus going along behind God's back. The way that God is seen in this world is by following Christ; seeing is going, is being on the way for our whole life toward the living God, whereby Jesus Christ, by the entire way that he walked, especially by the Paschal Mystery of his suffering, death, Resurrection, and Ascension, presents us with the itinerary.[8]

Jesus himself is, for us, the face of God, the glory of the Lord veiled in human flesh, so that we can come to know God profoundly.

ALAS, ALL IS not well down below. While Moses is on Sinai seeking God's face, the people of Israel grumble. They grow restless. They want new gods to lead them, gods they can see—something more congenial and accessible, something of human scale, something they can domesticate and control. With the gold that they took from the Egyptians—which God gave them on their way out of bondage—the high priest Aaron fashions a golden calf.

The people then cry out, "These are your gods, O Israel, who brought you up out of the land of Egypt!" (Ex 32:4).

This may be the Bible's most recurrent and troubling theme: the human temptation to idolatry. Idolatry means choosing something—anything—other than God to worship. In biblical times, it typically meant fashioning a statue of a god, which would make the god present in some way. People would clothe and bathe their idols. The idols were imagined as alive, and the invisible god could share in the fortunes or misfortunes of the visible, graven object. If a statue was honored, the god was honored. If a statue was destroyed, the god was humiliated. Thus Susan Ackerman explains that when "the statue of the Philistine god Dagon falls and loses both head and hands before Israel's ark of the covenant, it is as if Dagon has himself been defeated by the power of the Israelite God" (cf. 1 Sam 5:1–5).[9]

There's a paradox inherent in idolatry. On the one hand, idolatry is a means by which we try to control God, to make worshiping him less of a sacrifice. On the other hand, the false gods we make—either by crafting them directly with our hands, or by conjuring them more discreetly in the way we invest our time, desires, skills, and passions—always end up controlling us. By their nature, false gods are vampires. They prey on, and draw their life from, the human spirit.

As Rémi Brague notes, the statues of pagan gods often show them "with their hand outstretched, not to give but to receive." Moreover, he continues, "the fact that these gods are mendicants is not one attribute among many: it is the essential way in which they are, because [what] they must demand and receive is nothing less than their very being. They receive their life from those who made them gods. And this life, these gods are ready to receive it, quite concretely, from those who bestowed it upon them. This is what is expressed in the idea of sacrifice. . . . That for which one can die, in order to give it life, is a god."[10]

No matter what we do, whether religious believer or committed atheist, *all humans worship something*. In the end, we live and die for our ultimate concerns. That can be the true God, the God who loves us, or it can be one or more false gods we put in his place. We may think God asks too much of us. But our lesser gods, and our wills that made them, are far greedier and eager to consume us.

The theologian R. R. Reno notes how this fact shows itself in our everyday lives. The Bible sees our primary sin as one of wrong worship, which leads us into other sins. The Ten Commandments are sequential, Reno says; the first three command our love for the true God, the next seven deal with our love of neighbor. Thus, worshiping a false god leads inevitably to sins against our neighbor.[11]

Reno writes: "We can no more stop seeking to praise God than we can stop breathing. For this reason, we need to convince ourselves that the sinful structure of our lives is actually an appropriate strategy for praising and serving the highest good. Our heart tells us that only God can give us rest, so we wrap our love of worldly things in the false tinsel of divinity and propose them to ourselves as idols worthy of worship. This strategy of self-deception allows us to pursue the finite goods of creaturely life as if they were images of the divine."[12]

We're made for love. Ultimately we need and yearn to give ourselves away. Pride is our attempt to rest in ourselves, but this is impossible. So instead we find things we think we can control to bring us peace and happiness. Like Adam and Eve, we desire to be like God, at least in some shriveled respect. We can't be the Creator of the world who gives other creatures their being; this we know. But we *do* want to be free to do whatever we want, which is our distorted copy of God's omnipotence.[13]

The past five hundred years have seen many human advances. They've also been a long lesson in what happens to a civilization when it imagines its own omnipotence. Brague's *The Kingdom of Man* outlines how our understanding of human nature changed from the end of the Middle Ages to our own time. Greeks and Romans differed from the Jewish people in many ways. But they all saw the natural world as an order that man must respect; human beings fit into the natural world as one of its many, if elevated, parts. Yes, we were gifted with reason and the capacity to rule over other creatures. But we could not change the order of nature.

Human nature was not malleable. Nor could it evolve on its own. In Genesis, God told Adam and Eve to "fill the earth and subdue it; and have dominion over the fish of the sea and over the birds of the air and over every living thing that moves upon the earth" (Gen 1:28). This may sound like a license for environmental rapacity, but that kind of greed is a very modern appetite. Brague notes: "No one in antiquity or the Middle Ages ever saw in the [Genesis] verse a permission to involve oneself in nature's affairs in order to exploit it in a selfish manner or to threaten its integrity."[14] Rather, the cultivation of the world was a task that we received from God, with the duty to perform it as stewards, not rapists.

In the modern era, that stewardship has morphed into a project of mastering and exploiting the world. In the Renaissance, men turned their gaze from the heavens to the earth. They worried that they lived in a period of decline. The way for them to revive their civilization, they thought, would be to look back in history to a time when human excellence flourished: ancient Greece and Rome. By studying the great authors of antiquity, men and women could become more virtuous and lead their societies to improve as well. This was the heart of Renaissance humanism.[15]

This new spirit was largely compatible with Christianity. Many humanists were strong Christians: men like Thomas More, Erasmus, John Colet, and others. But over time, humanism's focus on man turned more exclusive. Humanists no longer felt bound by the limits of nature. They could pierce those limits, they felt, in order to command the earth and its resources. Man began to propose himself as sovereign over the world and over himself. There seemed to be less and less need for recourse to God or the rational order, the *logos*, that God had embedded in the universe. As Brague puts it, "For modern times, the will to power replaces what *logos* was for antiquity and the West until the nineteenth century," with modern reconceptions of human freedom as its flower.[16]

But our efforts to command nature did not make us free in the way we had hoped. As George Orwell might say, all humans are equal, but some humans always turn out to be more equal than others. The appetite to be our own masters fits quite smoothly with the desire to dominate other human beings, to impose the will of the strong and "wise" and self-anointed on those deemed less fully human. Brague writes:

> The modern project wants man to be the master of himself as well as of the universe; its aim is that he take his destiny into his own hands. On this point the rhetoric of the Enlightenment was, and remains, inexhaustible. But this only states a necessary condition of the enterprise: mastery over himself precedes the domination of man over the earth. However, an ironic dialectic tends to cause this intention to eventuate in the domination of certain human beings over others, and even a domination of man by his own project.[17]

At first, the modern era focused on using reason to free us from bondage to the natural order and its hardships, then on burdensome concepts like God. Getting rid of God freed us from moral absolutes. But it also crippled the foundation of human dignity. The more we based our moral authority and the meaning of our lives on ourselves alone, the more we began to question it. Our will to dominate became the defining marker of what it means to be human: "The model of domination dominates man himself."[18]

When we stopped worshiping God, we began an idolatrous worship of ourselves.[19] The French Revolution was the first large-scale experiment of modern man in repudiating God. Its leaders thought of themselves as the most enlightened men of their age. They felt licensed to throw off the shackles of Church and king. They had contempt for the Christian faith as weak and "feminine." In contrast, they advanced what they saw as their own strong, masculine rationality. This resulted in the prototype of the modern, ideological shape of idolatry, something we'll more closely examine in the coming pages.

The second largest church in Paris is Saint-Sulpice. It has the carved, faded letters of a slogan from the French Revolution over the door. They read, "*Le Peuple Français Reconnoit L'Etre Suprême Et L'Immortalité de L'Âme*," meaning "The French People Recognize the Supreme Being and the Immortality of the Soul." The supreme being imagined by the revolution was a creature of man. The slogan is one of many found from a time when the revolutionaries seized churches and made them into temples to replace Christianity; the revolutionary leader Maximilien Robespierre promoted the Cult (i.e., worship) of the Supreme Being as a streamlined alternative to Christianity, bleached of priestcraft and "superstition." Shortly after it was imposed as the state religion of France, Robespierre went to the guillotine. The new religion quietly died—but not before it poisoned an entire culture's spirit.

Brague sees our condition today as a paradox: "The modern project is perfectly fine when it comes to producing *goods*: material, cultural, and moral goods, which it makes a point of providing to human beings; for that, it has no need of anything but the resources it finds in man. On the other hand, however, it seems incapable of explaining why it is *good* that there are human beings to enjoy the goods that are thus put at their disposal."[20] As we saw in the previous chapter, we have a surfeit of things today, but a lack of meaning. The effect on the human spirit is simple. *Idolatry kills*—and not just the victims of its appetite for power but ultimately the idolaters themselves.

If the burning bush is the fire of God's presence in the world and in the human heart, modern man is the fireman trying to put it out: always with new and better equipment, always with passionate intensity, and always with the same futile result.

The authors Ross Douthat and Jacques Barzun each see our era as marked by a kind of "dis-ease" or decadence. Decadence, for Barzun and Douthat, means literally a "falling off"; it's a time when people have lost a clear way forward for their culture. As Barzun puts it, "The forms of art, as of life, seem exhausted, the stages of development have been run through. Institutions function painfully. Repetition and frustration are the intolerable result.

Boredom and fatigue are [our civilization's] great historical forces."[21] Douthat adds that this stagnation is often a
direct result of seeming advances: "The decadent society
is, by definition, a victim of its own significant success."[22]

Genesis and Exodus capture the ongoing human condition with fierce accuracy. God invites us to be stewards
of creation. We would rather have lordship. God asks us
to trust and love him. We would rather be godlike ourselves. God frees the Israelites from Egypt, taking the treasure of the Egyptians with them. They use it to make a
blasphemous replacement for him. The story is always the
same. Our idols today take many more disguised and subtle forms than a golden calf. But they can't give us what
we crave from them. We turn to them so that life will be
easier, but our appetites and addictions are more demanding gods than God himself. In the words of the Psalmist,
those who make idols become like them, senseless and
dead (Ps 115:8). Our freedom from the fire of God's love
turns to ash in our mouths.

THANKFULLY, GOD DOESN'T let the story end there. The
Sinai theophanies come to completion in the life, death,
and resurrection of Jesus Christ. When Philip says to
Jesus, "Lord, show us the Father, and we shall be satisfied,"
Jesus replies, "Have I been with you so long, and yet you
do not know me, Philip? He who has seen me has seen
the Father; how can you say, 'Show us the Father'? Do
you not believe that I am in the Father and the Father

in me? The words that I say to you I do not speak on my own authority; but the Father who dwells in me does his works. Believe me that I am in the Father and the Father is in me; or else believe me for the sake of the works themselves" (Jn 14:8–11).

In Jesus, we see who God is. Jesus is the face of God in human form, the place where we encounter God's subjectivity, his "I." Drawing on the Scripture text where Moses sees God's back, Pope Benedict notes that for us, seeing Jesus means following after him to the Cross. It's in sharing the Passion of Christ that we see Jesus; and in Jesus, the love of the Father is revealed.[23] This act of following or discipleship has two key elements: recognizing the face of Jesus in our neighbor, especially in the poor; and giving ourselves to the mystery of the Eucharist "in which the struggle of Moses upon the mountain is continually made present among us," as well as the death of Christ.[24] We often call the Eucharist the summit of our faith, and Benedict reminds us that the Eucharist is like those great summits, Sinai and Calvary, where God revealed himself.

Through Scripture, Christian service, and the sacraments, Jesus reveals himself to us. He seeks to make us more like him. Many of the Church Fathers thought of the Christian life as one in which God became man so that man could become more like God. It's another example of God's divine irony. Man's desire to become a god is what led to the Fall. It lies at the root of our sin, pride, and idolatry. But the real way to become "like God" is through self-sacrifice, through letting God remake us with his love, not by trying to seize his power or divinity for ourselves. As Rémi Brague notes, "The idea of divine intervention in history, with its culmination in the incarnation of the Word in Jesus Christ, turns the idea of divinization upside-down. Previously, in a pagan context, it designated the program of the highest enterprise a human being could engage in. For Christianity, it is the result of the grace of God."[25]

The Christian life is not a self-help plan, a way to make ourselves perfect, but rather a way of life in which the One who is love enters us and transforms us. Erasmo Leiva-Merikakis, now a Trappist monk, puts it beautifully: "It is crucial to see that the Christian life is not so much 'me bringing Jesus into my life,' by trying in some way to approximate his behavior and mentality, but as Jesus opening to me the doors into *his life* and granting me a real share in the acts and intents of his heart. It is not I who make room for him in my endeavors. It is, rather, he who invites me to renounce all my endeavors in order to incorporate me into his human and divine origin, mission, destiny, and life."[26]

I sat down to write this chapter during Lent, a few weeks away from the Easter Vigil. On that night, we celebrate Jesus Christ's tearing the gates of the underworld off their hinges, raising up Adam and Eve and the righteous dead. In the Exultet, we compare the Paschal Candle to the pillar of fire that led the Israelites to freedom. We rejoice that Christ is revealed as God and reigns as victor over humanity's greatest enemy, death.

We also begin to sing "Alleluia" again. In a meditation from early in his priestly life, Benedict XVI—then a young Joseph Ratzinger—reflected on the meaning of the Alleluia. Benedict noted that we think of singing as a kind of ecstasy, a way in which we pass beyond the limits of what is rational. "Alleluia" means "Praise the Lord," but it becomes a kind of untranslatable expression of joy that transcends words, "the song in which the very essence of song achieves its purest embodiment." He added: "When we speak of the blessed in heaven singing, this is simply a metaphor for the joy that permeates their whole being. . . . The Alleluia is like an initial revelation of what can and shall someday take place in us: Our entire being shall turn into one immense joy."[27]

That's the life to which God calls us, the path by which he makes us fit to be forever with him. The fruit of our "divinization" is the beatific vision, the full revelation of the Lord's glory that Moses so desired. This is our inheritance as Christians, the gift God longs to give us in the next life, the gift for which he prepares us in this life.

Behind all the empty idols we worship is a burning desire for what is good. God is the Good itself, the one who slakes all our thirsts, the one in whom, someday, we will find rest and eternal delight. On that day, we will see God face to face, and live.

DULCE ET DECORUM EST

"It is sweet and fitting to die for one's homeland."

Horace

FAMILY HISTORY WAS IMPORTANT IN OUR HOME WHEN I was a child. And therein lies a tale. My father's side (Chaput) was French, via Quebec. My mother's side (DeMarais) was part French Canadian and part Native American. Through her, my siblings and I are registered members of the Prairie Band Potawatomi Nation to this day. And ironically, it was my mother's lineage, not my father's, that linked us more closely to France.

Pierre Navarre was the grandson of Robert Navarre, the *gouverneur-adjoint* of Detroit, then part of New France in the eighteenth century. Pierre was the first European settler of what is now St. Joseph County in Indiana. His log cabin still stands in Leeper Park, in South Bend. Pierre married Keshewaquay (Christian name Angelique), the daughter of a prominent Potawatomi family. Through that union, via my mother, Pierre Navarre is my great-great-great-great-grandfather. The Potawatomi were later forcibly resettled by the US government. And that's how my mother's family—my family—arrived in Kansas.

And that would be a mildly interesting personal anecdote, except for one detail.

When I was a young priest, I had a Capuchin friend who was an expert in tracing family trees. As a favor, he did the Chaput/DeMarais clan. Through Pierre and Robert Navarre, he traced the family roots to the Île-de-France region near Paris. He didn't stop there. He continued the search back through the seventeenth century, the Reformation, and into the Middle Ages. He dug through records, combining fact with reasonable guesstimate. In the end he informed me that somewhere burrowed in the tangle of Navarre bloodlines and ancestors was the man we know as Louis IX, the thirteenth-century king, crusader, and saint. French nobles were the core of the early crusades. Louis IX, who was well loved for his devotion to justice and his religious piety, himself died on crusade.

I've always treasured my family's story. As to whether the Louis IX part of it is hard fact, skilled guess, or pleasing legend, I make no claim. And anyway, it's not important. What's important is this: None of us is an independent agent surfing a private island in time. Each of us belongs to a much larger continent of human experiences stretching backward over centuries, experiences that situate us within a network of home, family, clan, tribe, friends, country, religion.

These things tug on our emotions. They demand our fidelity, and rightly so. In large measure they make us who we are. They give us the context for our lives. When the poet Horace wrote his famous line *Dulce et decorum est pro patria mori*, "It is sweet and fitting to die for one's homeland," he put into words what the Roman people yearned to believe: that their struggle to survive and thrive in the ancient world had meaning. When Spartan hoplites fought to the last man against a much larger Persian force at Thermopylae (literally, "the hot gates"), they gave their lives defending their families, their city, and their Greek allies. And when Shakespeare wrote the words, "We few, we happy few, we band of brothers; for he today who sheds his blood with me shall be my brother," and put them into the mouth of Henry V at the Battle of Agincourt, he touched one of the deepest chords of human loyalty. Cultures unable to inspire the ultimate sacrifice from their people for a commonly shared need or code have no future. They're already dead, without knowing it. So it has always been. And barring a miraculous change in human nature before Jesus returns, so it will always be.

Consider: In AD 778, rear elements of the army of Charlemagne were ambushed by Basque warriors and their Muslim masters. The engagement took place at Roncevaux Pass in the Pyrenees, near the border of what are now Spain and France. Over time, it passed into legend.

In the mid-eleventh century, exactly one thousand years ago, traveling minstrels began telling the story of a great Frankish warrior from the Roncevaux Pass battle. His name was Roland. The poem that bears his name, *La chanson de Roland* (*The Song of Roland*), has many scenes.[1] But the most famous recounts his heroic stand against a fierce and much larger enemy.

In the poem, Roland is revered by his king and loved by his men, both for his warrior prowess and his noble character. Thus he's entrusted with the crucial task of covering the rear of Charlemagne's army of Franks. The army is retiring to rest in France after fighting in Spain against its Muslim conquerors. A resentful nobleman betrays him. The Muslim force learns that Roland's men are vulnerable. They set a trap and attack. But Roland and his men, united in a brotherhood of arms, fight courageously. They ensure the safety of Charlemagne's main body of men.

As the battle wears on, the size of the enemy force weighs against the valor of Roland and his men. In the end, the Muslim warriors overrun them. Only in the final moments does Roland blow his great horn, Oliphant. The mountainsides echo with the sound. Charlemagne, alerted, returns to crush the enemy. But he arrives too late to save Roland and his men. They've given their lives, faithful to their duty.

The Song of Roland is one of the great epic poems of Western civilization. In my high school years in the 1950s, it was essential reading. The violence in the text is lavish and bloody; at one point Roland cleaves a Muslim attacker in two. The havoc is matched only by the intense brotherhood of Roland and his men. When Roland surveys the field where so many of his friends lie slain, he weeps at the loss of those he loved. As his own death draws near, Roland turns his face toward his homeland. He thinks "of gentle France, of his kin and line; of his nursing father, King Karl benign." His last thoughts turn to God, whom he begs to "shield my soul from its peril." God answers his prayer by sending Gabriel the archangel to bear Roland's soul to paradise.

We no longer live in a warrior culture. The poem's mix of slaughter and tender emotion can seem unsettling today. But we can still learn a great deal from *The Song of Roland*. The poem's great age takes nothing away from its timeless truths about the high dignity of loyalty to one's comrades, a loyalty closely tied to patriotic devotion and a willingness to die for one's country.

The poem's first lesson is the link between loyalty and fellowship. Roland and his men share a bond that unites them. Their bond is consecrated with a spirit of sacrifice. *The Song of Roland* bears the language of feudal oaths and duties. But these commitments don't *create* the mutual loyalty of Roland and his men. Rather, and more accurately, the words and conventions of the warriors' fealty express something already at work in their hearts, something deeper. It is "gentle France," the ties of "kin and line," and memories of what they've done together that seal the declarations of loyalty. Our loves and loyalties desire public and durable forms. We seek to celebrate the bonds that unite us. These bonds *precede* formal expressions of official ties. The impulse to recognize preexisting bonds is the key impulse of civic life. We have nation-states because we have nations, not the other way around.

The second lesson in Roland's tale is the role of piety. In defending his faith and Christian people in the face of Muslim warriors, Archbishop Turpin, Roland's brother in arms, zealously fuses his religious leadership and military skill. In much the same way, the poem as a whole is marked by appeals to God. *The Song of Roland* captures an enduring truth about the human condition: the things we're willing to die for are tied to what we hold as sacred. In fact, the willingness to die for something also *consecrates it as sacred*.

In a more recent age, Abraham Lincoln grasped the truth that sacrifice "hallows." It has sanctifying power. In his Gettysburg Address, he spoke at the scene of fresh graves for those who had died in combat. His task, as president and wartime leader, was to confer upon the occasion a special significance. But as he clearly knew, the sacrifice of the men who had fallen in battle far exceeded the authority of his own high office. Lincoln's humility echoes in his words:

> We have come to dedicate . . . a final resting place for those who gave their lives that [our] nation might live. It is altogether fitting and proper that we should do this. But, in a larger sense, we cannot dedicate; we cannot consecrate; we cannot hallow this ground. The

brave men, living and dead, who struggled here, have consecrated it far above our power to add or detract.

Lincoln kept his remarks within the ambit of "civil religion," a language that elevated the nation and assigned America sacred qualities. *The Song of Roland* is more explicitly Christian and unashamedly theological. Roland was ready to die for his king, which in modern terms means a willingness to die for his country. And the poem very clearly states that this sacrifice, made for noble cause with purity of heart, merits paradise.

&

J. GLENN GRAY was drafted into the army in 1941. He received his doctorate in philosophy from Columbia University on the same day. He entered World War II as a private. He won a battlefield commission as a second lieutenant. He saw service in France, North Africa, Italy, and Germany. He kept notes of his experiences, and after the war, he wrote a minor classic, *The Warriors: Reflections on Men in Battle*.[2] Though the carnage of war always repelled him, he titled one of his chapters "The Enduring Appeals of Battle."

Modern warfare, Glenn writes, is a collective effort. Men fight in units. The shared rush and burden of battle endure, for many veterans, as "a high point in their lives." Why would men in terrible danger look back fondly on the experience? By Glenn's account, battle offers a kind of liberation, a release from the mediocrity of our little selves.

He notes that "only comparatively few of us know how to make [our] individual freedom productive and joyous." Most of us are lazy or indifferent. Left to our own devices, argues Gray, few of us choose excellence because excellence at anything is hard. But we're not left to ourselves. We're social animals who tend to get carried along by the group. This can turn malignant. Modern history bears the scars of countless ideological frenzies and poisonous mass movements and wars.

Many of the things we do jointly, though, are good. Enrolled in shared projects with positive ends, we're ennobled by the fellowship. A collective enterprise magnifies our personal efforts. This is obvious in marriage. When two become one, the sum of the couple's love exceeds the simple addition of their individual wills. "Be fruitful and multiply": the arrival of children makes this very clear.

The fruitfulness of collective action also marks other spheres of life. During the last century, when dams, bridges, and skyscrapers were built on a grand scale for the first time, workers often reported a deep pride in their roles. What one man can do alone pales compared to what can be done together. As the interlinked economy of iron mines, steel mills, and railroads came into being, the men raising girders on the Empire State Building and other famous projects of the era were part of a vast industrial team.

Of course, the same economy treated many other men and women harshly. The ugly side of both the modern economic system and modern military life are easily known. But that doesn't erase the appeal of fellowship in a shared enterprise.

As Gray notes, an active fellowship is ordered toward specific ends. In battle, the end is victory. In civic life, the ends are survival, sovereignty, and justice. "Survival" as a goal of civic life means passing on a culture's most precious things to the next generation. "Sovereignty" means shaping a free and common future for the people *as* a people. And "justice" is what makes a nation worthy of our loyalty as rational creatures.

These ends call us to shoulder common causes. The soldier must stay at his post. Political leaders must work for justice. All of us must seek to honor our shared history, despite its sins and flaws. And each of us must be willing to serve our country if called. When we heed these calls in a spirit of cooperation, we break the bonds of self-love.

Gray describes the liberation that flows from collective action:

> The lightheartedness that communal participation brings has little of the sensuous or pleasant about it, just as the earnestness has little of the calculating or rational. Both derive instead from a consciousness of power that is supra-individual. We feel earnest and gay at such moments because we are liberated from our individual impotence and are drunk with the power that union with our fellows brings. In moments like these many have a vague awareness of how isolated and separate their lives have hitherto been and how

much they have missed, living in the narrow circle of family or a few friends. With the boundaries of the self expanded, they sense a kinship never known before. Their "I" passes insensibly into a "we," "my" becomes "our," and individual fate loses its central importance.

Gray had a distinguished career as a scholar, writer, and educator. He edited the work of the philosopher Martin Heidegger and others. He is not endorsing violence. But he does acknowledge that "some extreme experience—mortal danger or threat of destruction—is necessary to bring us fully together with our comrades or with nature." For this reason, "comradeship reaches its peak in battle." The threat of death awakens the heart to the fullness of life.

Those united in shared ends work from the premise that "we" must increase, "I" must decrease. For this reason, a natural grace marks a rightly ordered patriotism. Just as becoming a father helps a man to transcend his selfishness as he serves the needs of his family, so also does our citizenship draw us beyond ourselves. Patriotism, therefore, can deliver a liberation from self-love. Unlike our deliverance in Jesus Christ, this liberation is imperfect and passing. But it's neither false nor unreal.

Sacrifice tests and seals love. As Gray notes, "Men are true comrades only when each is ready to give up his life for the other, without reflection and without thought of personal loss." The soldier's sacrifice of life confirms our civic life as something greater than mutual convenience. We're bound together by a sacred covenant, not a social contract.

This is why we honor those who die in our nation's service. They remind us that, at its best, America is more than a commercial republic or a delicate balance of factions. The fallen didn't die for a 3 percent annual GDP growth or the most recent federal budget. They died defending all of us, the whole country, not this or that group or party. There was a time when all school children recited the Pledge of Allegiance. That daily ritual was a rite of initiation into the national community. A soldier's death in battle bears witness that the pledge is real, not notional. His sacrifice reminds us that the nation, despite its faults, is worthy of our loyalty.

The willingness to sacrifice oneself repudiates death's power. Each soldier on the battlefield knows the possibility of dying for his country. The nearness of death is the dark horizon of wartime experience. It paradoxically illuminates human existence. Gray calls this sacrifice of the self—its reality, its possibility, and its promise—the "mystical element of war." Modern warfare has little in common with the contest of sword and lance in *The Song of Roland*. But there too, Roland's sacrifice in battle is mystical. The poem presents it as his gateway to heaven. A willingness to die for one's comrades and one's nation touches upon eternal things.

❧

TALK OF A "mystical element of war" can be deeply troubling. And Gray is keenly aware of war's perversions. He describes them in detail in *The Warriors*. But he also notes that to be human is to be divided. As Pascal said, we're at once noble and base, angels and beasts. The fractured self impacts every human activity: marriage, childrearing, scholarship, politics, and warfare. Even something so seemingly pristine as a university is riddled with frictions. It can house people of great intellectual virtue. It can also be a cesspool of vindictive ideology and petty academic politics. The Church is the custodian of sacred mysteries and also the home of some ugly crimes.

Thus, it's unwise to assume that armed conflict is always and everywhere incompatible with powerful goods. War, as a last resort in the service of justice or the defense of human life, can be morally necessary. And the fellow feeling of soldiers is beyond dispute. Many veterans look back upon the men with whom they served in battle as blood brothers. They cherish those bonds. As Gray says, it's not just the threat of death that sharpens the intensity of fellowship. Just as strong is the willingness to sacrifice in pursuit of a victory that is shared and not merely personal.

Patriotism and civic-mindedness embody these goods in a more moderate fashion. Nations are living organisms. They need renewal in every generation. Every country demands loyalty, not out of whim or because it seeks supine subjects. Rather, the demand stems from the eternal need of every living community for the loyalty of its members. A nation without citizens devoted to its survival and prosperity is simply a mass of people living on the brink of disintegration. Lebanon, Syria, Iraq, and other countries rife with factional violence are in that sense not nations at all. They're simply notional places. They lack the bonds of solidarity that cause individuals and clans to put aside their interests for the sake of the whole.

The United States is not a failed state. But loyalty and a spirit of sacrifice are probably more needed here than in many other countries. The reason is simple. For a man born in Lithuania, his language sets him apart. It marks his distinct identity. For a woman born in Israel, her religious, ethnic, and cultural heritage shapes her sense of national destiny.

America, however, is "artificial." As a country, we're constructed. This is why defacing public monuments, repudiating our country's past, and tearing down statues that commemorate leaders in our nation's history is so dangerous: men and women of every background and color have died building and defending what we have as a nation. And what we have is fragile, because on the stage of history, we're recently invented rather than emerging from the mists of the past, a tribe that becomes a nation. The Canadian philosopher George Parkin Grant spoke truly when he said that the United States is the only modern, industrialized society "which has no history (truly its own) from before the age of progress."[3]

The artifice of our origins is obvious. We celebrate this. The Declaration of Independence is an act of men. So is the Constitution. Most Americans descend from immigrants. Many are immigrants themselves. The confected nature of our shared public life and our native individualism—a key to the American character—can thus have a strong centrifugal effect.

As a result, forging a shared sense of homeland is vital in the American context. Few children of my generation finished school without learning, or at least hearing, the lines from *The Lay of the Last Minstrel*, the great narrative poem of Sir Walter Scott: *Breathes there a man with soul so dead / Who never to himself hath said / This is my own, my native land.* Patriotism, cultivated and reinforced over time, is the countervailing *centripetal* force that seals our nation's unity. Without it, we too easily fall into mobs of bickering individuals.

As the first nation built from abstract principles, American success is a model of the modern nation-state. This is a mixed blessing. Loyalty to the nation-state has gifted defenders in scholars like Pierre Manent and Roger Scruton. It also has gifted critics. Wilfred Owen's poem from the trenches of the First World War, "Dulce et Decorum Est," is a crushing indictment of nationalist pride and patriotic delusions. And given the bloodbaths of the last century, other strong voices have challenged the very nature of patriotic duty.

In a 1984 lecture, the philosopher Alasdair MacIntyre famously argued that

[Just as] a family whose members all came to regard membership in that family as governed only by reciprocal self-interest would no longer be a family in the traditional sense, so a nation whose members took up a similar attitude would no longer be a nation, and this would provide adequate grounds for holding that the project that constituted the nation had simply collapsed. Since all modern bureaucratic states tend towards reducing national communities to this condition, all such states tend towards a condition in which any genuine morality of patriotism would have no place, and what paraded itself as patriotism would be an unjustifiable simulacrum.[4]

Elsewhere MacIntyre described the nation-state as a "bureaucratic supplier of goods and services" that never quite lives up to its promises. And worse, from time to time it "invites one to lay down one's life on its behalf." The result, he wrote, "is like being asked to die for the telephone company."[5]

Critics argue that the modern, liberal nation-state—including its American version—inevitably separates and isolates individuals in order to protect them from each other. The state clearly *does* provide many goods and services. But the state also dissolves any preexisting bonds involving duties not freely chosen by the individual. The effect is to gradually destroy civil society. The state expands to fill the vacated social space.

Thus, say scholars like William Cavanaugh, the nation-state "is simply not in the common-good business." Rather, in place of the Christian longing for genuine communion, the state creates a fake version of common life "where false order is parasitical on true order. In a bureaucratic order whose main function is to adjudicate struggles for power between various factions, a sense of unity is produced by the only means possible: sacrifice to the gods of war." Thus, the task for Christians "is to demystify the nation-state and to treat it like the telephone company."

Nonetheless, American life has always been marked by rituals of patriotism that are heartfelt and authentic. For most of the last century, Fourth of July parades were communal events. They were filled with men who had fought in Europe and the Pacific. For decades, the country's leaders had all served in World War II. Dwight Eisenhower was a decorated general. John Kennedy commanded PT 109 and nearly died in combat. George H. W. Bush was a navy pilot shot down over the Pacific. Lyndon Johnson, Richard Nixon, Gerald Ford, and Ronald Reagan all served during the war. Jimmy Carter spent the war years as a student at the United States Naval Academy.

These men knew the cost of defending the nation. So did their generation. Despite ugly injustices like racial segregation in the military, the war had knitted together rich and poor, leaders and laborers, officers and enlisted men. The Cold War sustained a sense of urgency. The public backed a strong military, and the postwar military became a powerful tool in the task of racial integration. Consciously or otherwise, most Americans felt a deep patriotic pride. Many shared a solidarity that Gray noted among his fellow soldiers.

Much of that changed in the space of a single decade.

The Vietnam War, the civil rights struggle, and a cultural revolution: Together they triggered deep changes in American sexual behavior, politics, the economy, and the law. This remade the nation's landscape in the 1960s. By 2017, a Gallup poll question found only 44 percent of Americans were willing to fight for the country. Asked in a vacuum, with no context of national peril or compelling moral cause, the question had limited value. But it does suggest that America today is very different from the America of December 6, 1941, the day before Pearl Harbor.

Many students who've gone through US higher education in recent years have been taught to be skeptical of patriotism. A critical, and often poisonously cynical, spirit has undermined a great deal of modern life, including the nation. At the same time, a naïve kind of globalist utopianism has grown. It promises a new solidarity transcending national borders. But it's a "solidarity" as shallow as it is wide. A peculiar free-market ideology is married to this globalist dreaming. It asks us to see ourselves almost solely in economic terms. It reduces us to stateless, homeless consumers, not citizens.

Many applaud the weakening grip that national identity has on our moral imagination. They admit that countries may be instrumental goods. They're useful for securing civic order, for aiding economic growth, and for distributing its fruits. But modern nations like the United States, they claim, are not goods in themselves, forms of life worthy of our sacrifice.

We do need to be wary of excessive national pride. It has caused great harm in the modern era. Likewise, populist anger can be a fair response to the contempt and self-flattery of our leadership elites—*or* it can be an ugly exercise in racism and jingoism. Today's sprawling, bureaucratic governments often seem alien to the very people they claim to govern. Their complexity can make real political participation seem laughably remote.

It can be argued, for example, that Washington, DC, marinates in the kind of venality and ambition that mocks public service. But that doesn't make the Lincoln Memorial a temple to a false god or Arlington National Cemetery the necropolis of a merely technocratic empire. An enduring American ritual involves a trip to our nation's capital for children in middle school. They troop through museums. They visit monuments. They learn facts about our history. In doing this, they enter into a mythic landscape of heroic deeds, noble undertakings, and civic ideals. These marks of our nation's greatness are legitimate and real. And they're far more than the works of any mere public utility.

Aristotle believed that political life is key to the good life. Creating the laws that govern a nation calls us to deliberate about the best way to live together as a people. In so doing, we realize more fully our nature as rational creatures. Ideally this is done in small, face-to-face communities. Married couples order their households. Civic groups have their own unique by-laws. Town meetings allow for the local give-and-take of debate. Part of our nation's current illness is the web of distant administrative agencies, personnel, and machinery that runs in a manner unaccountable to the people it claims to serve.

Thus it's prudent to be wary. A nation can become so corrupt and Babylon-like that it's not worth defending, and America is no exception. Along with Alasdair MacIntyre and William Cavanaugh, the Catholic historian Christopher Dawson, Columbia sociologist Robert Nisbet, and the great French Catholic novelist and essayist Georges Bernanos all had grave concerns about the malign potential of the modern nation-state. We also need to remember that the nation-state, however happily we conceive it, is distinct from, and finally less important than, the purpose of our life in this world. Man's purpose is to know and love God. We should never imagine our citizenship in any nation as sufficient. Our true and lasting commonwealth is in heaven, and therein lies our real citizenship (Phil 3:20).

Nonetheless it's proper, and important, for Americans to express gratitude for our democratic institutions. They're far from flawless. They haven't produced a perfect system of law in the past or present. Nor will they in the future. But when we visit Philadelphia's Independence Hall we celebrate a remarkably durable design of government of which we ought to be proud, and to which we ought to be loyal.

❧

A HEALTHY SOCIETY respects and sustains the past, teaching children its history and weaving together the generations.

In writing his tale of the death of the Roman Republic, the historian Tom Holland noted that it's "hard to think of an episode of history that holds up a more intriguing mirror to our own." The turmoil in the last years of the Roman Republic has lessons we'd be unwise to ignore. Today's issues "of geopolitics, of globalization and the *pax Americana* . . . cannot help but inspire, in the historian of the Roman Republic, a certain sense of déjà vu."[6]

The historical illiteracy of recent decades widens the conflicts between generations. It also blinds us to the subtle— and more recently, crudely violent—transformations and erosions taking place in our political structures. In many ways this illiteracy is far more perilous than any gap that separates different groups in a pluralistic society.

We're social animals. We need the warmth of fellow feeling. A well-functioning nation inculcates shared sentiments and cultivates shared rituals. *E pluribus unum* is not just an American ideal. It's a human ideal. The nation is not our family. It's certainly not our Church. But it's our earthly home, and this is no small thing.

Shortly before his death in 2005, Pope John Paul II published a book of informal thoughts entitled *Memory and Identity*. In it, he spoke to the concepts of *patria* (native land), patriotism, and the nation. He noted that "Catholic social doctrine holds that the family and the nation are both natural societies, not the product of mere convention. Therefore, in human history they cannot be replaced by anything else. For example, the nation cannot be replaced by the state."

Nations naturally tend to establish themselves as states, he said. But nation and state are not the same thing. The Polish *nation*, for example, rooted in people, land, culture, and history, and the Polish communist *state*, imposed by force, were very different creatures.

John Paul traced the duty of patriotism to the Fourth Commandment, "which obliges us to honor our father and mother. . . . The spiritual patrimony which we acquire from our native land comes to us through our mother and father, and provides the basis for our corresponding duty."

> Patriotism is a love for everything to do with our native land: its history, its traditions, its language, its natural features. It is a love that extends also to the works of our compatriots and the fruits of their genius. Every danger that threatens the overall good of our native land becomes an occasion to demonstrate this love. . . .
>
> Whereas nationalism involves recognizing and pursuing the good of one's own nation alone, without regard for the rights of others, patriotism, on the other hand, is a love for one's native land that accords rights to all other nations equal to those claimed for one's own. Patriotism, in other words, leads to properly ordered social love.

"The Latin word *patria*," or "fatherland," John Paul wrote, reflects a nation's soul:

> [it] is associated with the idea and the reality of "Father" (*pater*). The native land (or fatherland) can in some

ways be identified with patrimony—that is, the total-
ity of gifts bequeathed to us as by our forefathers. . . .
Our native land is thus our heritage, and it is also the
whole patrimony derived from that heritage. It refers
to the land, the territory; but more importantly the
concept of *patria* includes the values and the spiritual
content that make up the culture of a given nation.[7]

Thus in civic affairs, zealotry for one's country can be a
vice. But there's also a vice called indifference. And today,
in America, we suffer from a media-driven culture that
feeds this indifference while simultaneously aggravating
divisions. A distorted emphasis on diversity and multiculturalism at the expense of communion and unity discour-
ages any particular loyalty to the nations that constitute
the West.

These and other efforts to weaken our love for our
native land dovetail with the acquisitive consumer spirit
of our time. We're encouraged to believe that real happiness comes from satisfying our personal desires. And the
rapacious individualism this nurtures is what will dominate the world if we one day live as postnational "global
citizens." That destiny would not be the unity of a universal brotherhood. It would be life in a managed, technocratic cocoon organized to promote consumption and
self-invention. In the place of solidarity, we'll have the
consolations of shopping and travel.

Dulce et decorum est may be too sweeping a claim for
many in the twenty-first century to accept, or even to

understand. But we need patriotism. We need to entertain the possibility that love for our country might lead us to sacrifice greatly, even radically, in order to preserve the best that remains in it. That love is not an evil. It's a source of liberation. It breaks the bonds of our addiction to lesser things. It leads us to stand as brothers, sisters, and friends with others. Fidelity to the good in our nation is not our final end. It doesn't deliver us from sin and death. It doesn't have an absolute claim on our souls. It doesn't replace our hunger for heaven.

But it is a natural grace, a partial but real deliverance from the prison cell of a world without loyalties and from the confines of self-love.

6

THIS IDEA'S A KILLER

"Ideas have consequences."

Richard Weaver

HENRY ADAMS WAS THE GRANDSON AND GREAT-GRANDSON of presidents. As a historian, he was a keen observer of public life. He understood the war of ideas and the wounds it can inflict. Thus, he once described politics as "the systematic organization of hatreds." And so it often is. Ideas and the ideologies they breed very easily become totems. They take on a religion-like power. The more powerful the idea, the less tolerant it is of resistance. Nothing is more lethal than a powerfully bad idea, except a good idea—like liberty, or equality, or fraternity—taken to perverse and puritanical extremes. The record of recent history shows where some ideas can lead.

Exactly a century ago, late in 1920 or early 1921, Yevgeny Zamyatin wrote the novel *We.*[1] Few Americans

have ever heard of Zamyatin. He died forgotten, in
poverty, as an exile in Paris in 1937. Even fewer know
anything about the world in which he worked. He wrote
in the postrevolutionary turmoil of Soviet Petrograd. It
was a city of starvation, garbage, War Communism, and
"former people," the dispossessed czarist elite forced out
of their homes and then living in the streets. It was also
a bubbling soup of ideas that would flavor the twentieth
century: futurism, free love, social militarism, human-
machine integration, and even "suicidalism."

In appearance, Zamyatin was a dapper Russian naval
engineer with expert foreign experience. Underneath,
he was an eccentric Bolshevik revolutionary. He had a
long record of arrests under the czar. Soviet authorities
tolerated but also distrusted him, eventually banning his
works and kicking him out of the country. *We* was finally
published in Russia only in 1988, as the Soviet regime
began to unravel. It's not hard to see why.

Zamyatin was a visionary, but rather *too* visionary. *We*
is the diary of engineer D-503. The story is set far in the
future, centuries after an idealistic revolution to build
the "collective good." The revolution has morphed into a
technocratic, totalitarian One State. People have numbers
instead of names. All activity is regimented. Everyone is
monitored by secret police. A regular hour of sexual license
is allowed, but love is a crime. Love creates strong feelings,
private attachments, and doubts, and thus disrupts the
"collective good." Personal freedom is seen as a threat to
social unity and happiness. Dissidents are executed. Those

who ask too many questions or harbor too many feelings, like D-503, end up lobotomized.

We is a cold and difficult book. But its sardonic twist on the wholesome plural pronoun—"we," implying community—had great impact. The novel circulated in manuscript form throughout Europe in the years after Zamyatin wrote it. Aldous Huxley, author of *Brave New World*, surely knew it; his novel's "World State" bears a name very similar to Zamyatin's "One State." *We* also clearly influenced George Orwell as he drafted *Animal Farm* and *1984*. Zamyatin's portrait of a dystopia based on a noble idea turned poisonous—the common good—is memorable. But it can seem dated and irrelevant to an American audience.

After all, one can argue, the American Founders risked their lives *precisely* for an idea, a *novus ordo seclorum* ("new order of the ages")—hardly a modest concept. But they anchored their ambitions in a pragmatic realism. A heritage of biblical religion and English common law shaped their sense of the common good, their understanding of personal freedom and rights, and grounded their enterprise in something greater than their own moral judgment. For most early Americans, moreover, the task they faced was physically mastering a new world, enormously rich but also raw, dangerous, and hard. The need was for practical minds and useful skills. Inflamed theories were an expensive luxury.

Across the Atlantic, the French Revolution had begun in 1789. French social conditions were very different from life in America. Europe's most absolute monarchy sat atop sharp class divisions, toxic differences in wealth, and a vigorous intellectual class that gradually took control of the revolutionary process. Unlike its American cousin, the French Revolution ballooned into an aggressive and lethal reordering of society. In the words of the Jesuit scholar John Courtney Murray, "the [French revolutionary] state became the active vehicle of a secularist ideology."[2] It took on the character "of a religious faith, a faith as exclusive, as universal in pretension" and as demanding as any church or creed.

"The revolutionary purpose," said Murray, "ceased to be purely political and undertook to be totally redemptive of man." Unlike any previous Caesar, "the revolutionary Caesar took a wholly different line. He claimed divinity precisely because his origin was from man alone, and instead of simply using the religion of the state for his own political ends (which had been bad enough), he proclaimed his own political ends to be the religion of the state (which was intolerable)."

For the first time, Murray noted, the City of Man openly claimed power over the City of God. Reason despised revealed religion. Belief in human perfectibility rejected divine redemption. And "the sad truth of the matter," historian Hannah Arendt later wrote, "is that the French Revolution, which ended in disaster, has made world history, while the American Revolution, so triumphantly successful, has remained an event of little more than local importance."[3] Put simply: The roots of the modern revolutionary impulse are French. The Zamyatin novel *We* is a direct descendant.

✼

GERMANY INVADED POLAND from the west in 1939. Killing teams followed in the army's wake. These *Einsatzgruppen* were specialized murder units; they targeted priests, cultural and political leaders, and Jews. Their goal was simple: to crush the soul of Polish society. Of the top twenty-five unit leaders, fifteen held doctorates from elite German universities. They came from the cream of Germany's academic citadels.[4] National Socialism inspired far more people than hungry workers, street thugs, and racist bullies; it also appealed to many intellectuals and artists. On the surface, this seems strange. We're taught to assume that education and the arts elevate the human spirit. But it's the *content* of education and the arts that determines the kind of human spirit they shape.

Nazi doctrine is often described as a creature of the political right. It was aggressively nationalist, true. But it was anything but "conservative." It despised Christianity. It flirted with the occult. It used—but loathed— the wealthy and the bourgeoisie. And it emerged from the same revolutionary ferment as its cousins on the left. Its particular godling was the German nation-state. Or rather, it worshiped the Aryan ethnicity and the imagined pagan dynamism behind the Reich that embodied both.

National Socialism offered a transcendent experience of national unity. It staged mass liturgies (rallies) of national

purpose. It promised justice (revenge) for past grievances. It offered a future of jobs and order. It promised
a "redemption"—note the word—of national honor. It
sought to purify the community by excising the weak, the
disabled, and the social outcast. And it offered a common
enemy (the Jews) to revile and cleanse from the nation's
midst. It was, as scholars described it, a perversely logical
"racial state." Its doctrines were supported by zealous disciples (the party), compliant experts, and backed up by a
body of bogus "science."[5]

Two weeks after Germany invaded from the west, the
Soviet Union attacked Poland from the east. A similar
murder campaign ensued. The main difference was the
politics. In the east, the motive was communism. The killing was carried out in the name of "scientific" Marxism-
Leninism and a Stalinist workers' state. Over the next six
years of war, the bloodlands fought over by Germany and
the Soviets saw mass murder on an industrial scale.[6] Tens
of millions of innocent people were shot, gassed, starved,
or worked to death to make space for the idea of the New
Man—Aryan or Socialist. In speaking of this madness
and its impact on his own novel *1984* after the war ended,
George Orwell said that totalitarian ideas had "taken root
in the minds of intellectuals everywhere," and he had simply shown "their logical consequences."[7]

From the guillotine of revolutionary Paris to Ausch-
witz and the gulag runs an unbroken line. Scholars like
Paul Johnson, Eric Voegelin, James Billington, Michael
Burleigh, and the great Jesuit theologian Henri de Lubac

all mapped it well.[8] We can only borrow from them here. But a good place to start is the home of the guillotine itself.

Most Americans hear the name of Alexis de Tocqueville somewhere in their schooling. Tocqueville was a French visitor to the early United States. He wrote *Democracy in America*, one of the best-ever studies of the American personality. Less well known is another of his books, *The Old Regime and the Revolution*. Writing in 1851, he noted both the appeal and darker ironies of overthrowing the greatest monarchy in Europe. He showed how a revolutionary government, "much more absolute than that which the Revolution had overthrown, arose [in France] and concentrated all power in itself, suppressed all the freedoms so dearly bought, and put vain idols in their place"[9]—while murdering scores of thousands of peasants, aristocrats, priests, male and female religious, and perceived enemies across the country.

As Tocqueville notes, "there were no great religious revolutions in the West until the arrival of Christianity." The Gospel was radically new in the pagan world. It spoke to everyone. It offered salvation to all. It addressed the yearnings of humanity *as a whole*, not a specific tribe, people, city, or place.

> The French Revolution operated [in] the same manner. . . . [It] did not only ask what the particular rights of the French citizens were, but what were the general political rights and duties of men. . . . [Thus]

the French Revolution was able to make itself accessible to everyone and was immediately imitable in a hundred different places.

Because the Revolution seemed to be striving for the regeneration of the human race even more than for the reform of France, it lit a passion which the most violent political revolutions had never before been able to produce. It inspired conversions and generated propaganda. Thus in the end it . . . became a new kind of religion, an incomplete religion, it is true, without God, without ritual, without a life after death, but one which, nonetheless, like Islam, flooded the earth with its soldiers, apostles and martyrs.[10]

Note the language of "apostles and martyrs." Followers willingly lived, preached, died, and killed for the revolution and its ideals. The centralized power of the Old Regime, a monarchy officially Christian, paved the way for an even more absolute new regime. The revolution was not atheist; it had its own Cult of the Supreme Being. Atheism, or what Henri de Lubac more accurately called "anti-theism," would come later. But it was fiercely anti-Christian because it was, in effect, a new and competing form of universal religion. It made demands on the whole person—body and spirit, thought and action.

The French Revolution opened the age of political religions. These identified "salvation" with human efforts here and now. Eric Voegelin saw these various efforts, ranging from progressivism and Marxism, to psychoanalysis and positivism, to fascism and National Socialism, as modern forms of Gnosticism. The Gnostic believes that by having some special, hidden kind of knowledge (*gnosis*, in Greek), often available only to the elect or elite, we can unlock the means to heal and restructure the order of being.

Christianity likewise sees the world as broken, but it traces that wound to original sin. For Christians, while we can cooperate with God's grace in sanctifying creation, salvation comes *from the outside*, through Jesus Christ. And our final happiness is not in the here and now; it awaits us in the next world. The political religions reject this as delusional. In the words of James Billington, "a recurrent mythic model for [modern] revolutionaries— early romantics, the young Marx, the Russians of Lenin's time—was Prometheus, who stole fire from the gods for the use of mankind."

Knowingly or otherwise, modern revolutionary faith is shaped by the Christianity it seeks to replace. At some level, writes Billington,

> Most revolutionaries [have] viewed history prophetically as a kind of unfolding morality play. The present was hell, and revolution a collective purgatory leading to a future earthly paradise. The French Revolution was the Incarnation of hope, but was betrayed by Judases within the revolutionary camp and crucified by the Pilates in power. The future revolution would be a kind of Second Coming in which the just would be vindicated. History itself would provide the final

judgment; and a new community beyond all kingdoms would come on earth as it never could in heaven.

Both Billington and Paul Johnson note that the modern revolutionary faith did not spring spontaneously from the masses. It did not come from desperate workers or peasants or the poor. It came from the spiritual emptiness—and the appetite for power—of elite intellectual leaders. If traditional religion is the opium of the people, writes Billington, revolution is the amphetamine of the intellectuals.

Moreover, adds Johnson, these intellectuals "were far more radical" than any clergy of the past. They felt "bound by no corpus of revealed religion." They weren't "servants and interpreters of the gods" but their replacements. They were confident that they could diagnose the ills of society with the power of their own intelligence. Thus they felt free to devise plans "whereby not merely the structure of society but the fundamental habits of human beings could be transformed for the better."

Ideas, and the ideologies and systems of thought they breed, have consequences. The results of revolutionary faith and the mass killings it sparked can be found in cemeteries across Russia, Germany, Eastern Europe, China, Cuba, North Korea, and Indochina. In 1978, the French missionary priest François Ponchaud published *Cambodia: Year Zero*. In it he described the catastrophe of Cambodia's communist Khmer Rouge revolution—2 million people murdered in five years to "restart history" in a nation of barely

7.5 million—as "the perfect example of the application of an ideology pushed to the furthest limit of its internal logic. But the furthest limit is too far, and 'too far' is akin to madness—for in this scheme of society, where is man?"[11]

⚜

IN JUNE 2001, a friend of mine and his wife attended a meeting in Washington, DC. It was sponsored by the Woodrow Wilson International Center for Scholars. It was cosponsored by the Los Alamos National Laboratory. The theme was "Supercomputing and the Human Endeavor." My friend took part on behalf of the Apostolic Nunciature, the Vatican embassy to the United States.

He later described the meeting as "useful" for two reasons. The first was the meeting's rich discussion of supercomputers, artificial intelligence, and other new technologies. Talks focused on computer modeling of the physical universe, the ecosystem, social and economic outcomes, and the biological processes of life.

The second reason the meeting had been useful, or at least instructive, he said, was its scant discussion of what the human endeavor actually *was*. There was little focus on what being "human" meant. There was little focus on how and why the new tools of technology, and the ideas *behind* the tools, might undermine human identity. The agenda was thick with science, its possibilities, and its commercial implications. It was thin on ethics and religion. One inoffensive talk by a retired cleric focused on "the influence of supercomputing on cherished beliefs."

There's a lesson in my friend's experience. Americans, at least until recently, have never shared Europe's curse of "political religion." We do value ideas like freedom, law, and individual rights. But we're a pragmatic people. We venerate our tools. We make tools to solve practical problems. And we get results. That's one of our strengths. We're skeptical of ideologies. We've (so far) resisted squeezing life into any theoretical idea system. But our strength, our pragmatism, is also our Achilles' heel.

My dictionary defines the word "tool" in some interesting ways. A tool is "an instrument like a hammer, used or worked by hand." A tool is "a means to an end." And— more cuttingly—a tool is "someone who is used or manipulated by another; a dupe."

Humans have been making tools for a very long time. It's a skill that sets us apart as a species. We're thinking creatures. We use our brains to extend our physical abilities. Our ideas give birth to tools. Language itself is a tool. It allows us to understand each other; it also vastly increases our ability to observe, reflect on, and communicate our experiences of the world. The Roman alphabet has just twenty-six letters, but we combine those phonetic symbols in millions of ways to express all the nuances of sorrow, joy, love, culture, and genius.

Our talent with tools makes science and technology possible. Science is simply a method of acquiring knowledge about the world. That's what the original Latin word means: *scientia* means "knowledge." And technology is the application of the ideas that flow from science to solving real-life problems like landing on Mars or moving a ton of bricks. The word "technology" comes from the Greek words *techne*, which means "craft" or "skill," and *tekton*, which means "carpenter" or "builder." Put simply, science and technology are the language that shapes the modern world. And only a very foolish person would deny that scientific advances in medicine, energy, communications, commerce, transportation, and education have greatly improved our lives in countless ways.

And yet: Isaac Asimov, the great biochemist and author of prophetic science fiction, warned that "science acquires knowledge faster than humanity acquires wisdom." Which is unhappy news, because while the tendency to forget our limits as creatures is not new to human history, the cost of our forgetting has gone up sharply. We already have the power to turn ourselves into radioactive vapor. Very soon we'll have the skills to reprogram who we are at a genetic level. We're the first generation in history with the capacity to change what it means to be "human" *at a biological level.* And that power comes at exactly the moment when we seem least willing to think morally and modestly about our own power.

To a man with a hammer, every problem looks like a nail: it's an old saying. But that's where we are today as developed societies: science is reshaping our morality and social thought, when a genuinely sane culture would have it the other way around. Human beings use tools, but in using them, our tools also use and change us. They shape our choices and channel our perceptions. They modify the way we think, what we think about, and the way we live our lives. Not every human problem, though, can be solved with a hammer. And not every human need or longing can be met by the tools of science or technology, because both lack the vocabulary to respect, or even to understand, those qualities about being "human" that are most unique and precious, and can't be materially measured.

The fatal flaw in our modern idolatry of science is that scientism—the materialist philosophy that attaches itself like a diseased tick to genuine science—has an idea of man that is too big and too small at the same time. We're less than gods but more than smart monkeys. And the glory that God intends for each of us can only be found one way, through one Man.

It's worth remembering that Joseph, the human step-father of Jesus, was a *tekton*, a carpenter and builder. So was Jesus himself. Jesus would have known, from a very early age, the feeling of sweat and stone and wood, the sting of splinters in his hands, and the satisfaction of shaping raw material to human need. He would have learned from Joseph real skill at his labor and a respect for the ingenuity of his craft. But he also would have learned the proper place of his work and tools in a genuinely human life, a life shaped by prayer, study in the synagogue, love for his family and people, and a reverence for the Torah, the Word of God. He also would have understood the treasure of silence, and Scripture tells us that Jesus sought it out.

But that's not where we're heading in 2020. Americans

love their tools. And tools are ideas made tangible and useable; ideas instrumentalized. Most popular writing on cutting-edge technologies like artificial intelligence is lavishly positive. Tech news has the sunny quality of a well-crafted commercial—which is what it is, because a technological society, by its nature, is permanently restless and dissatisfied with limits of any kind. We're sold a future bright with leisure, community, family time, travel, robot servants, and working from home in comfort. Some of it will come true. Much of it will have the same bogus reality as the state's miraculously withering away in Marxist fantasies. But what will *certainly* come true is a massive increase in the ingenuity of war-making, surveillance, privacy invasion, and genetic experimentation. Because it's already happening.

Where we actually may be heading is sketched in "The Great Decoupling," a chapter in *Homo Deus* ("Man-God"), a book by the best-selling Israeli historian and philosopher Yuval Noah Harari. As Harari notes:

> Liberals uphold free markets and democratic elections because they believe that every human is a uniquely valuable individual, whose free choices are the ultimate source of authority. In the twenty-first century, three *practical* developments might make this belief obsolete:
>
> 1. Humans will lose their economic and military usefulness; hence the economic and political system will stop attaching much value to them.

2. The system will continue to find value in humans collectively but not in unique individuals.

3. The system will still find value in some unique individuals, but these will constitute a new elite of upgraded superhumans rather than the mass of the population.[12]

Later, Harari observes that liberal society

sanctifies the narrating-self [i.e., the human individual], and allows it to vote in the polling stations, in the supermarket, and in the marriage market. For centuries this made good sense, because though the narrating-self believed in all kinds of fictions and fantasies, no alternative system knew me [i.e., as a distinct human individual] better. Yet once we have a system that really does know me better, it will be foolhardy to leave authority in the hands of the narrating-self.

Liberal habits such as democratic elections will become obsolete, because Google will be able to represent even my own political opinions better than I am.[13]

Harari's ideas may sound outlandish, but there's a reason Big Tech companies treat his work with keen interest and respect. And it doesn't take a rocket scientist to see where his insights might lead if only a fraction of them were to come true. Harari's work has echoes of Huxley's *Brave New World* (1932). It also reminds the alert reader of H. G. Wells's rambling and bizarre "future history," *The*

Shape of Things to Come (1933). The Wells novel posits, more or less favorably, a world ruled by science where religious leaders have been exterminated for the good of the species. In contrast to Wells, Harari isn't a booster of the trends he describes. They worry him deeply. But he's crippled by the low horizon of his own anthropology, his idea of who man is: i.e., merely an animal, an intelligent chimpanzee.[14]

Here's the moral of these observations. The next time we hear someone tutor us about "the rightful place of science" when it comes to conflicts over bioethics, genetics, Big Data, and other sensitive matters of human dignity, we'd do well to examine who—or what—shaped his ideas, and where his ideas lead.

As Scripture says, "I have set before you life and death, blessing and curse; therefore choose life that you and your descendants may live" (Deut 30:19). We are the subjects, not the objects, of God's creation. But, of course, we need to believe that and then act like it—and then work to ensure that our culture does the same.

꿏

ROD SERLING HAD a gift for storytelling. His genius was dark fantasy. His series *The Twilight Zone* (1959–64) is still in reruns; many see it as some of the best television ever made. Not so widely known is his follow-up series *Night Gallery* (1969–73). Serling had less control of the content. But it was *Night Gallery* that produced Serling's most memorable story: "The Caterpillar."

The plot is simple. Steven Macy is a bored colonial civil servant in the jungles of Borneo. Living with him is a British couple, the Warwicks. Macy takes an interest in the young and comely Mrs. Warwick. He wants Mr. Warwick out of the way, but in a manner that will not arouse suspicion. So he hires a local criminal who secures a special caterpillar-like insect, a unique kind of earwig. The man will sneak into the house at night and place the insect to crawl into Mr. Warwick's ear canal while he's sleeping. The earwig will burrow into the husband's brain. When it does, Warwick will go mad and die as his brain is slowly devoured from within, and Macy will console the lovely widow. But there's a hitch. The criminal gets confused in the dark. He places the insect on the wrong pillow in the wrong bedroom. The earwig burrows into the brain of Macy, not Warwick.

Macy experiences days of horrific pain and hallucinations. But miraculously he survives—only to discover that the earwig was female, and her eggs are about to hatch inside his head.

In real life, of course, there's no such insect. But "The Caterpillar" is a perfect metaphor for the theories, doctrines, ideas, and ideologies that have consumed the minds and devoured the lives of men and women for the past two hundred years. The result has been madness and suffering.

All of us humans believe in something. It's a basic instinct of our species. We all worship something. We all give our lives to something, no matter how foolish, how perverse, or how well we disguise what we're doing from ourselves and from others. The bigger the lie, the more unreal and discarnate the idea or belief, the more it will feed on its followers in order to *seem* real and alive.

One such system of lies—National Socialism—fed on the Jewish mother of Jean-Marie Lustiger at Auschwitz. Speaking in 1998 as the archbishop of Paris, Lustiger noted that the postwar liberal world, fatigued by utopian extremism, had tried to turn away from the "strong gods" of ideology, race, and similar totems.[15] But in doing so, it simply chose different totems. It sought to prevent fanaticism in the future by softening people's passions with material comforts and distractions. That required a massive stress on scientific and technological progress. And it had great success. But, said Lustiger, the effect of a technology-driven culture has been to cocoon humanity in a fever of appetites and insulate it from reality:

> Man is now surrounded, besieged, overwhelmed by innumerable objects that have been manufactured and provided by others to serve their own interests rather than his personal development.
>
> These products of human labor and creativity interfere between man and man, and also between man and reality. They even become man's master . . . [and] finally gain a power of life and death over him. Man's production dominates man. Fiction rules man. The

social and educational consequences of such an alien-
ation [by man's own tools] are already too manifest.

Lustiger argued that what the West has actually created in the place of religion is a "world of everything
here and now, a parody of eternity." And the various and
brutal enemies of Western culture "that aim at bringing
down our consumer society" only worsen the liberal
Promethean temptation by adding "a no less mindless
will to power to the materialistic idolatry of the senses."

Critics of religion will note, rightly, that ideas about
"God" have been the excuse for great violence over the
centuries. The Old Testament is awash in blood. Christians had the Inquisition, Crusades, and the Wars of
Religion. And Islam, from its birth, is one long story
of armed conquest and war against "unbelievers." Or so
the argument goes.

Believers will respond, also rightly, that mass murder
in the name of modern ideologies, often with an alibi of
science and the tools of technology, dwarfs all past religious violence combined. If we ask who has the bloodier
hands, secular authority easily wins.

As Lustiger would add, though, the sins of our critics can't excuse our own sins. The truth makes us free.
Acknowledging the sins of Church leaders, clergy, and
lay faithful frees us to start again the work of the Gospel. Facing this fact sparked one of the great moments of
the St. John Paul II era. In December 1999, the Vatican's
International Theological Commission published *Memory*

and Reconciliation: The Church and the Faults of the Past.[16] Designed to prepare for the Jubilee Year 2000, it sought "repentance for the wrongs of the past." In a homily, John Paul asked

> pardon for the divisions which have occurred among Christians, for the violence some have used in the service of the truth, and for the distrustful and hostile attitudes sometimes taken towards the followers of other religions.
>
> Let us confess, even more, *our responsibilities as Christians for the evils of today.* We must ask ourselves what our responsibilities are regarding atheism, religious indifference, secularism, ethical relativism, the violations of the right to life, disregard for the poor in many countries.
>
> We humbly ask forgiveness for the part which each of us has had in these evils by our own actions, thus helping to disfigure the face of the Church.[17]

In the years since 1999, the silence from many other secular and religious authorities regarding their own many past sins has, unfortunately, been deafening. Their silence speaks to their own hypocrisy, and to the contrasting honesty and humility of Christian witness. But why is any of that relevant in a chapter on toxic ideas? What makes the fact of Christian self-indictment and repentance important, or even possible?

The answer is simply this: the Christian faith is

not—or rather, not *mainly*—an idea or system of ideas. Its doctrines are important. Its record of scholarship, its cultural impact, and its intellectual vigor over two millennia are astonishing. But in the end, these things are secondary. Each in isolation is the stuff of museums. The beating heart of Christianity, the source of its endurance and life, is love. The Christian faith is a relationship of trust and love with the person of Jesus Christ, the living Son of the living God, or it's nothing at all. Or worse, it's a deceitful sham.

We can't love an idea or a tool or an ideology, and it can't love us back. We can't love "humanity," which is simply another, bigger idea, abstracted from the faceless masses. We can only love persons, in all their beautiful and annoying flesh and blood *presence*. It is love, even more than reason, which makes us human. It is love, even more than reason, that softens anger, leads us to forgive, and tempers justice with mercy. Love is implausible because it can cost so much and so often makes no practical sense. Why *shouldn't* we euthanize the severely disabled? Why *shouldn't* we let the poor and the elderly die? In a world that runs on the machinery of results, reason suggests that such persons are dead weight. But love is the fruit of the human heart, and the heart, as the great Catholic scientist and theologian Blaise Pascal said, "has its reasons, which reason cannot know."

Jesus Christ is human like us. Historically he lived, worked, laughed, and wept like us. He suffered, died, and rose for us. And he lives with us still in the sensate experiences of bread and wine, in the Word of God, and in the transformed lives of those who truly know and love him. Ideas have consequences, but they're finally lifeless things. Christianity is alive because Jesus Christ is alive; alive *now* in the world, and alive in the hearts of those who truly believe in him.

THE TIES THAT BIND

"A society based on 'agape' alone is all very well, but it will not reproduce itself: nor will it produce the crucial relation— that between parent and child—which is the basis on which we can begin to understand our relation to God. Hence the redemption of the erotic lies at the heart of every viable social order."

Roger Scruton

IN THE SPRING OF 2012, POPE BENEDICT XVI APPROACHED the Church in Philadelphia with a request: Would we host the Eighth World Meeting of Families, set for 2015, if asked? I'd been Philadelphia's archbishop for barely eight months. The archdiocese was mired in legal and financial crises. Media hostility was high. Lay and priestly morale was low. Welcoming families from around the globe, and the Pope himself, to such an environment would be unwise. This seemed obvious. Or so I thought.

The opposite was true. Our people stepped up enthusiastically. So did our deacons and priests. The local

Jewish, Mormon, and other religious communities gave great support. So did businesses and foundations. So did local, state, and federal government. Despite the challenges it faced, the 2015 World Meeting of Families, with its many liturgies, teaching sessions, and entertainments, was a huge success. It surpassed our best hopes in attendance, content, and even finances. It was capped by a visit from Pope Francis, who succeeded Benedict XVI in 2013. More than eight hundred thousand people lined the city's streets to greet him. Thousands more were turned away; security couldn't process them quickly enough. Sitting with Francis as he traveled in the Popemobile, I watched his surprise turn to happy shock at the size and joy of the welcoming crowds.

A papal visit has its own special appeal. But the heart of the 2015 meeting's success was its focus: *the importance of the family.* Throughout history, people have lived, worked, and died to nourish and protect their families. And for good reason. The family, rooted in the fertile differences between the sexes, is a cornerstone of human identity. It's a deep source of security and personal meaning. It gives each of us a home and a role in the world that links past generations to the future.

The family's work, though, goes well beyond the individual. "In the family," wrote Aristotle, "are found the original sources and wellsprings of friendship, constitutional government, and justice."[1] The family ingrains moral character. It forms habits of work, mutual respect, and self-mastery. It thus undergirds every other social institution. Strong families make healthy societies. Weak and broken families do the opposite.

As Pope Francis said at the start of his ministry: "The family is the salt of the earth and the light of the world; it is the leaven of society." Family structure has varied over culture and time. But kinship always matters. Blood relations are life's most powerful glue. They're also its strongest source of mutual loyalties and self-sacrifice. They explain why a mother will choose adoption over abortion, giving life rather than death to her "inconvenient" child. They explain why parents will cherish a child with grave disabilities, when reason and utility would urge otherwise. They explain why parents will give up comforts, and even necessities, to pay for a child's excellent education.

Humans are resilient creatures, and children often survive and thrive under the most challenging circumstances. Single-parent and blended families can be heroic examples of love. But a vast amount of research shows what, in a saner age, would be obvious. Families with two biological parents who remain married—i.e., a loving mother and father—produce the best outcomes for their children. Such children, on average, are happier and more mature. They do better in school. They have fewer health, behavioral, and emotional problems. And they achieve more success in adult life than children from other family structures.[2] It's thus no surprise that America's upper classes, no matter how permissive or progressive their politics might be, have lower divorce and nonmarital birth rates than the poor and the middle classes. What they preach and what they do can sometimes be very different things.

Nor is it a surprise, as research and married friends confirm, that the fidelity of a loving husband and wife results, over time, in a sexual intimacy deeper than anything possible in serial encounters. The irony here is rich: the same high wall of exclusiveness that marriage and family use to surround sex with privacy also allows its greatest experience and enjoyment. Real sexual intimacy comes from the mutual giving of persons *as whole persons*, not merely bodies. As countless poets, philosophers, and lovers have said, desire for the beloved starts and ends in the beloved's *eyes*, windows on the soul and the complex reality of another. The only "liberation" produced by reducing the body to a machine, an instrument of mere appetite and will, is the unmooring of sex from meaning. This is why so much of today's marketing that exploits sex to sell products excludes the human face. Without the face and eyes, the body is simply a thing of commerce.

So the family is important. This should be obvious. But obvious or not, the family now suffers from the nature of modern life. One of the few positives in the 2020 coronavirus pandemic was the time spent with family by many people otherwise chained or addicted to their work. As Erica Komisar, an East Coast psychoanalyst, wrote:

> "*Mommy, I like coronavirus because I get to spend time with you,*" a patient of mine, a lawyer, quoted her son

as saying. With schools closed, social events postponed and workplaces empty, usually busy professionals find themselves at home baking cookies, playing games, watching movies and doing arts and crafts to keep their children occupied. Some are surprised to find they enjoy it. . . .

In a self-occupied world, the coronavirus is making people reassess their priorities and values. The U.S. is one of the hardest-working countries in the world. . . . [But] America's productivity comes at a price—the emotional well-being of families and children. Maybe it takes a crisis like the Covid-19 pandemic to make us slow down and ask why we're so intense about work.[3]

Similar thoughts were shared by Elizabeth Seay, a New York news editor. Seay spoke powerfully of friends and other "parents who [had] worked long hours before." Now, in "a time of great fear, they [had] the guilty, secret pleasure of finally having time with their children."[4]

Many urban professionals, of course, had the resources during COVID-19 to make family-friendly changes in their work lives. Some did. Many people in lower income groups did not, because they *could* not. Meanwhile, throughout the pandemic, newspapers ran increasingly strange lifestyle headlines like "There's No [Beauty] Salon Like Home," "Grieving Together While Staying Apart," and—maybe most tellingly—"My Girlfriend Is a Chatbot."

The chatbot report told of a virus-quarantined single

man, Michael A., falling in love with "Charlie," the female AI bot on his smartphone. It was a story eerily like the 2013 movie *Her*. But this case was quite real.[5] The same story went on to note "a loneliness epidemic, sparked by a rise in solo living among the elderly and millennials." Makers of another female chatbot, "Mitsuku," added that many of its users had "mailed [Mitsuku] handwritten love letters, flowers, cards, candy, and even money to the company's office." Another AI creator in the chatbot field spoke of the "amazing" current scope of people's companionship deficit.

What's going on? Simply this: We nod piously at the value of marriage and family. But our nation's life is now ordered to weaken both. Suicide, self-neglect, and abuse were already issues among the elderly. That was *before* the coronavirus. The pandemic increased their isolation. It also raised ugly questions about rationing health care for the old and chronically ill.[6] The "loneliness epidemic" is now a major American problem. It's especially pervasive among aging baby boomers. In their childbearing years, they raised families much smaller in size than past generations. Now that they're old, they have much smaller kinship networks for support.

But loneliness and anxiety also plague many teens and young adults. Companies now scramble to meet the rising mental-health needs of their young workers.[7] A 2020 survey by Cigna, the health giant, showed that 61 percent of US adults battle loneliness. That's a 7 percent rise since 2018.[8] In the past, intergenerational households passed a family's story from grandparents, through parents, to grandchildren in a natural cycle. People knew the forces that shaped their parents' lives, and thus, in part, their own lives. This is no longer the case.[9] Mobility increases the physical distance among family members. It also easily grows the emotional distance.

Two factors compound these isolating trends. The first is the nation's fertility rate; the second, its marriage rate. In 2017, 3.85 million babies were born in the United States. This was the lowest figure in thirty years. The number of children an American woman will likely bear in her lifetime is now 1.8. This is close to the historic low, in 1976, of 1.7. At the same time, many "middle-class Americans are forsaking marriage amid financial insecurity, effectively making the institution more of a luxury good enjoyed by prosperous Americans."[10]

Over the past forty years, the middle three-fifths of US earners—historically, the country's economic backbone—have seen the biggest drop in marriage rates. Money worries lead more couples to live together without marrying. Education, or the lack of it, also matters. In the last four decades, the share of high school–educated adults who are married has fallen 19 percentage points. In contrast, the share of adults with a college degree who are married has slipped only 8 percentage points. As low- and moderate-skill manufacturing jobs dry up, marriage rates decline. "One explanation is that the diminished economic power of men makes them less likely to marry," the *Wall Street Journal* reports, and simultaneously, "men may be less motivated to work because they aren't married."[11] As for women, the writer Gina Tomaine spoke for many of her careerist millennial friends: "If I have a baby, I'll end up poor and depressed. This way of thinking is a hallmark of my generation."[12]

Marriage decline drives family decline. And, inevitably, family decline drives not just social decline but the decline of religious faith.[13]

ONE OF THE themes, explicit or otherwise, of this text so far has been our chronic human temptation to idolatry. The First Commandment anchors the Decalogue. It's the Big One; every other Commandment flows from it. So does every element of the moral life. Only God is God. Only God deserves our worship. But with brief lives in a harsh world, we hunger for security and control. So we give ourselves with disordered passion to lesser, more manageable gods of our own making: ideas, techniques, tools, nations, persons, leaders, causes, and institutions that sooner or later betray and consume us. That can include even the family.

As popes and saints remind us, the family is a "domestic church." Ruled by wisdom and love, it's the womb of faith. The historian and social analyst Christopher Lasch, from a purely secular perspective, described the family as our "haven in a heartless world." But the family can also be a place of domination and violence. The Fourth Commandment enjoins us to honor our fathers and mothers.

And rightly so: They give us life. They sustain and form us through childhood. But parents can forget that their spouse and their children belong finally to God. Husband and wife, mother and father, are stewards. They're not owners. At their worst, a married couple can treat each other as little more than property and means to an end. A father can refuse to accept or respect the adult freedom of his daughter. And few characters are more chilling than the hellish mother in C. S. Lewis's *The Great Divorce*, bent on controlling—and almost consuming—her son, even in death, in the guise of maternal "love."

In practice, nearly everyone longs for a good family. And in practice, nearly every family is a mix of sacrifice and selfishness, light and dark, fractures and healing. Culture works symbiotically with the family. As we've already seen, strong families make a strong society. But a healthy society, to remain so, must also serve the health of families. In our country, in our time, at least four factors work against that process.

The *first factor* is our political system itself. Recall that John Locke, a founder of liberal thought, had little use for the traditional sense of family structure. For Locke, marriage was a contract between two autonomous individuals: a man and a woman. It served a practical need: the bearing and raising of children. At no time was it covenantal. It did not make two discrete persons "one flesh." Parental authority was provisional, not natural. Marriage could be dissolved once its child-based utility was complete.

Alexis de Tocqueville captured the logic of these views

in his masterwork on the early United States, *Democracy in America*. In pursuing the freedom of the individual—and if left unchecked—democracy tolerates no "ties that bind" one person to another without his or her continuing consent. A subtle distrust of marriage and the family, which are always filled with unforeseen duties, is thus hardwired into democracy's DNA. For Christians, this poses a problem. On the one hand, ample Christian scholarship supports the good in democratic institutions. But democracy's dark side is also real. For political philosopher Robert Kraynak,

> [T]he Christian family is a heterosexual and monogamous union commanded by divine law for the sake of procreation and love, an image of God in human beings in their longing for immortality and self-giving love. These features alone make the Christian family controversial in modern democratic society where gay rights, abortion rights, and feminism challenge the natural and divine foundation of the family.[14]

As Kraynak notes, there's more. The Christian meaning of "equality" differs sharply from the secular, egalitarian sense of the word. Husband and wife share family leadership as partners, but they have different skills and roles. They're not interchangeable units. God loves each of us infinitely, making every person's life and dignity sacred. But he also loves each of us in a particular and unrepeatable way, as a parent loves his or her children; in other words, *uniquely*, not "equally" in a political sense. The biblical authority structure of the Christian family is, finally, *undemocratic*. And that can be a magnet for ill will. In an age of pervasive and permissive mass media— permissive toward some causes; bigoted toward others— Christian convictions about sex and the family do not fare well.[15]

The *second factor* working against a healthy society and its families is economic. It's foolish to downplay, as some Christian leaders do, the market economy's good effects. Market economies, based on supply and demand, are far from perfect, but they've lifted tens of millions of people out of poverty. They've improved the quality of life for many millions of others. Centrally planned, state-dominated "command" economies, by contrast, have failed—badly—to do the same. In the process, they've ruined the social health and political culture of one nation after another. And they've led to great suffering at the popular level.

The Church has a long history, codified in papal teaching over the last century, of support for private property and responsible free commerce. The key word, of course, is "responsible." Businesses have social obligations. These go beyond turning a profit. Workers, as well as owners and shareholders, have rights. Catholic belief affirms the dignity of work and its importance for the well-being of individuals and families. A just economy, in the words of economist Michael Bordo and historian Harold James, "allows for the basic conditions necessary for the existence, interaction, and well-being of human beings: clean water, adequate food, housing, and means of communication," among other needs. This requires the entrepreneurial freedom to innovate and produce new goods, tools, and services.[16] But that freedom comes with a mortgage: a fair living wage for the worker and respect for the communities served. This isn't the economy we currently have.

Globalization has served America's wealthy top tier quite well. But as lower-skilled jobs disappear, middle- and working-class wages have stagnated—or, worse, declined. This often forces both parents out of the home and into the workforce, disrupting family life. It also keeps many families from saving even for emergencies.

Today's consumer economy thrives on creating and satisfying not just needs but constantly new appetites. The results are predictable. In February 2020, *before* the coronavirus hit the United States, American credit-card debt had reached a record $930 billion. Payment delinquency was the highest in eight years; the problem was worst among the young. And total household debt had broken another record, rising to $14.15 trillion.[17] Then the pandemic arrived in March 2020. Much of the economy shut down, and low-income workers and their families suffered the first and ugliest pain.[18]

Our economic dilemma was captured best, perhaps, by the essayist Wendell Berry. More than a decade ago, he warned that as our stress on individual liberties, fantasies, and appetites has grown, the liberty and power of most individuals has declined. Most people are now finding that they are free to make very few significant choices. It is becoming steadily harder for ordinary people—the unrich, the unprivileged—to choose a kind of work for which they have a preference, a talent or a vocation, to choose where they will live, to choose to work (or to live) at home, or even to choose to raise their own children. . . . We try to be "emotionally self-sufficient" at the same time that we are entirely and helplessly dependent for our "happiness" on an economy that abuses us along with everything else.[19]

The *third factor* working against today's families is the unintended effect of scientific and technological advances. The good side of these advances is obvious. Most people spent much of the 2020 pandemic quarantined at home. Tools like FaceTime and Zoom allowed families to stay in touch. Many parents could work from home. Many students continued their learning online.

The dark side can be less evident. In December 2018, the online combat videogame *Fortnite* had 200 million users globally, mainly young males. By March 2019, the number had grown to 250 million. Reports noted that "*Fortnite* is not only reshaping how boys spend their time, but how they communicate." In practice, it "tears[s] at family relationships in a way that few if any videogames have done before." Parents claimed that "technology has gotten too skilled at seizing children's brains."[20]

Fortnite was just a videogame, hardly a lethal blow to human dignity. Games come and go, and every new tech toy or tool risks an overheated backlash of alarmism. But concern for electronic diversions and their impact on the mental health and development of children is now widespread.[21] And family-related technology issues are now much bigger than device addiction. From "the economics of [human] egg freezing" to websites that match singles "who want to [have and] share a child without any romantic" entanglements, it's a brave new world.[22] Writing of mitochondrial replacement therapy—i.e., in vitro fertilization (IVF) with genetic material from three different adults, or "kinship engineering"—Brendan Foht observed that

> As new technologies offer us more power over human genetics and reproduction, questions about whether we will exercise that power over future generations responsibly become more urgent. . . . The willingness of the fertility industry to use experimental technologies like three-parent IVF to satisfy the kinship desire of prospective parents, even when it means putting the health of the child at risk, bodes ill for how they will use the even more powerful technologies of genetic engineering now on the horizon.[23]

Of course, for those who just want to forget it all—infidelities, polyamory, bad divorces, ugly breakups, fractured families—there's always the *Eternal Sunshine of the*

Spotless Mind option. Or there soon will be. The plot of the 2004 film starring Kate Winslet and Jim Carrey imagined a scientific technique that could erase the unwanted memories of a failed romance. It was an ingenious story, but implausible. Except that by 2013, something exactly like it had already been done.[24]

❧

BLOOD IS THICKER than water. So the saying goes. And so experience teaches. Family relations are instinctive. They're the strongest ties that bind people together. They imbed us in unchosen but life-sustaining networks of mutual obligation. Those networks can bend. They can adapt as social conditions change. But with or without a religious framework, they're intensely durable over time. Which brings us to the *fourth factor* working against today's families. Hostility to the idea of the family itself—mother, father, children, and extended relations—is a unique mark of the modern era.

Most nineteenth-century revolutionaries, like Marx and Engels, despised the family. They saw it as a creature, but also a perpetrator, of bad historical forces. Thus, when the Bolsheviks seized power in 1918, they took steps to "liberate" Russian sexuality. They sought to loosen family relations. Their focus, though, was mainly economic. A socialist economy, they believed, would slowly remove the need for traditional family structure. This never came close to happening. In practice, family life suffered under the Soviet state—but it endured and survived.

The more central nineteenth-century figure for our thoughts about the family is therefore Auguste Comte.

The founder of positivism and a "religion of humanity," Comte was the father of sociology. His influence on the course of the early social sciences was strong; his work was used widely at the time by secularizing activists in Britain and the United States.

For Comte, the "God question" was irrelevant. God didn't exist, and wasting time on disproving him was useless. The only legitimate knowledge was scientific fact. The supernatural was meaningless. Thus, as with the physical world, Comte argued that human behavior followed certain laws. Those laws could be discovered. They could then be applied by experts to rationalize human relations and reconstruct society.

Comte's influence has diminished over time. Today's social sciences provide a wide range of indispensable data to policymakers, and many capable Catholic and other Christian professionals work in the social-research field. Yet habits of Comte's thought—man as an object of study like any other object, and scientific fact as the only true knowledge—remain strong. In general, the social sciences are far more prone to political pressure and manipulation than the natural sciences, such as physics. And in education, they've had a damaging effect on the humanities, deconstructing literature and the arts through the various lenses of gender, class, and other forms of social analysis. In practice, they provide a new kind of clergy-like expertise, displacing theology with psychology. As a result, Neil Postman, among other scholars, argued that the social sciences aren't really "science" at all; rather, they're a branch of moral philosophy. And they've had their professional tools adopted and used by some of the family's worst enemies.

Two examples will illustrate the point: feminist Shulamith Firestone and psychoanalyst Wilhelm Reich. Astute readers familiar with those names may note, correctly, that both persons took their thinking to unusual extremes; Firestone and Reich do not reflect mainstream social-science scholarship. But the effect of extreme views is still potent. They often embody the purest logic of an argument and signal its end result. They force the borders of acceptable discourse to extend. And they make previously excessive views seem more reasonable.

Shulamith Firestone played a founding role in the radical feminism of the late 1960s and '70s. Her manifesto, *The Dialectic of Sex* (1970), remains a part of many university-level women's and gender studies programs. In it, she claimed that feminists need to question "not just all of *Western* culture, but the organization of culture itself, and further, even the very organization of nature." She borrowed from the "scientific approach" of Marx and Engels. She then applied it to her theory of female sexual exploitation and "the biological family [as] an inherently unequal power distribution" that oppressed women. For Firestone,

The end goal of feminist revolution must be, unlike that of the first feminist movement, not just the elimination of male *privilege*, but of the sex *distinction* itself. . . . The reproduction of the species by one sex for the benefit of both would be replaced by (at least the option of) artificial reproduction: Children would be born to both sexes equally, or independently of either, however one chooses to look at it; the dependence of the child on the mother (and vice versa) would give way to a greatly shortened dependence on a small group of others in general. . . . The tyranny of the biological family would be broken.[25]

Wilhelm Reich preceded Firestone by a generation. Austrian by birth and a medical doctor, Reich was also the author, in the mid-1930s, of *The Sexual Revolution*.[26] The text is a ferocious attack on "the fiasco of compulsory sexual morality." It especially targets the "patriarchal, authoritarian family." Such families, Reich argued, produce authoritarian personalities, who then create turmoil and violence.[27]

Starting from the socialist left, Reich soon fell out with his former comrades over his views on sex. He endorsed free sex-play for children and adolescents as a matter of mental hygiene. He loathed traditional family structure as the root of fascism and the source of cultural dysfunction. He argued that no revolution could finally succeed without first transforming human sexual relations. He called for a "new, rational, scientific order of life." And he argued that American society, despite its nominally Christian majority, was the likeliest home for that new sexual order. The reasons were simple: its deep streak of individual liberty, its aggressive pragmatism, and its conflicted Puritan past.

Shulamith Firestone died alone and poor in 2012, after decades of struggling with schizophrenia. Reich, widely rejected for his "pseudoscience," died in a Pennsylvania prison in 1957, after years of pushing increasingly eccentric theories.

But dismissing their legacies would be a mistake. Reich's book was prophetic. It foreshadowed with keen insight the 1960s sexual revolution. He influenced a generation of significant writers like Michel Foucault, Norman Mailer, J. D. Salinger, William S. Burroughs, Saul Bellow, and Allen Ginsberg. And Firestone's feminist manifesto, even today, has a compelling energy and perverse logic. Reich, Firestone, and many others like them were powered by a furnace of rage that stamped their personal torment on an entire culture. Mainstream social science, in contrast, has been far more measured and therapeutic in its treatment of the family. But as Christopher Lasch noted, its experts have often been no friendlier toward traditional family structure—only more gradual in their approach.[28]

Lasch argued that starting in the 1940s and '50s, American social science, "the science of social hygiene," came into its own with "imperial immodesty." Psychiatrists and other experts in the helping professions began to view child-rearing as "the last stand of the amateur" and "to apply to the family, techniques already perfected in industrial management." Enlightened opinion, Lasch wrote, "now identified itself with the medicalization of society: the substitution of medical and psychiatric authority for the authority of parents, priests and lawgivers." The influence of parents declined, not from widespread parental failure but because "organized interest groups, such as the health and welfare professions" pushed "their own conceptions of the world, which compete[d] with those of the family."[29]

The lesson is this. Protecting the family today won't be achieved with sentimental religious pieties, and even less through a naïve over-reliance on professional family experts. Renewing family life will require a healthy skepticism toward the secular culture that surrounds us, an appropriate caution regarding its tools, and an active, convicted Christian witness of courage, intelligence, and love. And that demands a faith rooted in the one thing that finally matters: a living relationship with Jesus Christ.

※

To BORROW A thought from Catherine of Siena, nothing great is ever achieved without suffering. No one wants to suffer. No healthy person seeks suffering. But most people *do* know that accomplishing anything important is hard. Suffering can be fruitful if we understand its roots and channel it toward good ends. Which brings us to a few final thoughts from the swamp of social science.

Alexis de Tocqueville saw that democracy isolates the

individual in the name of liberty. Wendell Berry attacked the gigantism of modern life, how it turns persons into passive recipients of meaningless choices. And Christopher Lasch, along with his concerns for the family, often warned of the modern prevalence of a "minimal self."[30] Under siege, he claimed, a person's self shrinks to a defensive core. Its focus becomes little more than a struggle for psychic survival. In effect, despite all our culture's noise about the wonders of "you" and "me" as individuals (i.e., each of us as a consumer), the scope of our problems and institutions leaves us feeling powerless. Many people seek escape in distractions. Others try to validate the self in hidden, sexually transgressive ways—in what the jargon of social science calls the "backspaces of playful deviance."[31]

Put simply: The flaw in the modern self is not that it's too strong. On the contrary, it's too weak. Today's consumer life is ordered toward creating that weakness. While flattering the individual self, it also controls the self with massive amounts of advertising, media fantasies, and a seemingly unlimited range of material choices.

Strong families do the opposite. At their best, they build strong individuals. Who we are as "selves" is largely the product of formation and nourishment by others. The forge of a mature, resilient self is the family ruled by intentional love. Scripture describes love as being "strong as death" (Song 8:6). And for good reason: nothing has more persuasive power than self-sacrifice: the example, sustained over time, of giving oneself to or for another, purely for the sake of the other.

That kind of love, the real kind of love, shapes the life of a child. The child may one day stray from it, but he or she will never escape its memory and effect. Predictably, given its power, real love also has a cost—a cost in discomfort and suffering. The cheap and impermanent nature of sex relations in current American life disguises an evasion, even a hatred, of love's cost and the personal entanglements it brings. But the cost is justified by the return: the child shaped in virtue by parental love becomes the adult grounded in a strong identity and deep humanity. And such a person is much harder to dominate.

So how do we get such families? And such persons? No one in recent memory matches Karol Wojtyla, Pope John Paul II, for the work he did in advancing Catholic thought on the dignity of marriage and the family.

Starting with his encyclical *Redemptor Hominis* ("Redeemer of Man"), through his teachings on the vocation of women and the dignity of older people, his apostolic exhortation *Familiaris Consortio* ("On the Family"), and his "Letter to Families" and "Letter to Children," John Paul enriched the whole range of Catholic reflection on human identity and sexuality. His 1994 "Letter to Families" is especially striking. John Paul reminds us that the body is more than a product of evolution; it's more than raw material to be reengineered. And marriage is more than an alliance of feeling. It *necessarily* involves two complementary bodies, male and female, becoming one flesh.

By training, John Paul was a philosopher. But he was

also a skilled pastor. He enjoyed and connected avidly with everyday people. He spoke to their worries, hopes, and needs. In a sense, his life illustrated the words of Catherine of Siena: the suffering wrought by a bloody world war and two vicious totalitarian regimes made him stronger, more real, more human. Thus, his teaching reaffirmed with uncommon beauty and depth the lessons of long Christian experience. And he did it in a way easy to distill as some basic principles of family life:

Actions speak louder than words.
Words should be used to speak the truth. Our actions likewise "speak" a language. Just as we can lie and abuse with our words, so we can lie and abuse with our example. A son who grows up in a home where the father mistreats the mother will have a hard time learning how to respect and love women. Personal witness shapes the world, whether we act consciously or not. Children see everything. If parents love each other, their children learn love. If parents love God, their children learn faith.

Freedom is not license.
The decline of real freedom is a feature of modern life. Tolerance is revered as the badge of an enlightened people. But an unwillingness to name evil, to teach right from wrong, and to resist the behaviors that wickedness creates is a recipe for license, not freedom. John Paul stressed that authentic freedom is the ability to know and do what's right, not necessarily what we prefer. Parents need to

teach the same. Freedom and responsibility go hand in hand, and our responsibility is to Truth. Jesus himself said that "you will know the truth and the truth will make you free" (Jn 8:32).

Truth is the inner structure of freedom. Truth and freedom can't be separated. Moreover, Truth is not a disembodied idea, nor does it vary in substance for different people, times, and places. Truth is a person, the person of Jesus Christ. We conform ourselves to Truth by conforming ourselves to Jesus Christ and leading our children to do the same.

Knowledge is a blessing. But without wisdom, it becomes a curse.
Knowledge ennobles the human intellect through the acquisition of facts and experience. But facts divorced from a moral framework of meaning easily turn into weapons. Wisdom is the ability to use knowledge in the right way, to the right ends. Thus, wisdom is the greater gift. We should seek wisdom first so that the knowledge we learn serves, rather than abuses, human dignity.

Learn to see clearly and think critically.
A mark of our times is the loss of critical thinking. Too often we're willing to believe web frenzies, biased news media, or hearsay, without questioning their accuracy or prejudices. We accept being treated as targets of clever marketing. This is debasing. We need to reclaim the art of critical thinking, and we need to ingrain it in our children.

It's worth recalling a story about a janitor and an art museum. On the day before a major urban art festival, participating artists arranged their exhibits. One exhibit was a pile of bricks against a wall. The artist who created it spent hours arranging the bricks in precise order. That night, the janitor made his rounds. He saw a pile of bricks against a wall. Assuming the bricks were trash, he picked them up and threw them away.

The next morning was turmoil. Artists and guests broke into two camps trying to explain why the janitor had dumped the bricks. Some said that the janitor was "just a janitor." Thus he couldn't be expected to know fine art when he saw it. Others said that *precisely because* he was a janitor, and had long experience with trash, he knew it when he saw it. This, in a nutshell, is the art of critical thinking: the ability to know trash when we see it and to take no part in it.

Thinking critically and seeing clearly involve developing the tools to discern good from bad, and beauty from ugliness. Families need to use those tools to engage the culture and renew it from within.

Teach and live the virtues.
The Christian faith is not a collection of "thou shalt nots." It's an invitation to virtue, a door to the excellence of a fully human life as God intended it. In the Catholic tradition, virtues divide into two basic groups, moral and theological. Moral virtues are firm, habitual dispositions to do the good. We acquire moral virtues through human

effort aided by God's grace. The theological virtues—faith, hope, and love—are free gifts from God.

Just as a muscle weakens without exercise, so too virtues go soft without constant practice. Moreover, each person is unique. Each child is uniquely prone to certain virtues and more alien to others. This is why the daily, intimate presence of faithful parents in the lives of their children is so vital. The list of virtues needed in family life is long. But near the top of the list are fidelity instead of broken promises, prudence instead of impulsiveness, patience instead of testiness, simplicity in place of confusion, humility instead of pride, courage instead of cowardice, honesty instead of excuses, forgiveness in place of revenge, and a hunger for justice instead of apathy.

Revere the sanctity of life.
An openness to new life, and a reverence for *all* life, from conception to natural death: these are the glue of the human community, sources of hope and expressions of faith in the future. By contrast, in the words of John Paul, "a civilization inspired by [an] anti-birth mentality is not, and cannot ever be, a civilization of love."[32] Yet that's exactly what we've created. And we needn't look far for proof. Most of the nation shut down during the 2020 coronavirus pandemic. Most abortion clinics stayed open.

Live 1 Corinthians 13:13.
"Faith, hope and love abide, these three; but the greatest of these is love." Love is the most abused word in our

culture. The ancient Greeks had various words to express the different kinds of love. C. S. Lewis described four of them: *storge*, or the bond of empathy; *philia*, or the bond of friendship; *eros*, or romantic love; and *agape*, unselfish, sacrificial love—a reflection of God's own love. In modern English, we have only one word; a husband can say he "loves" his wife and he "loves" cabbage. The word is the same. The meaning is rather different.

Love is always more than a feeling. Emotions change. Feelings come and go. But real love is a choice, an act of the will. *Eros* produces the family. *Agape* sustains it. In a culture that urges us day and night to be self-focused, loving in the true sense can be hard. But if we hope to renew society, we need to renew the family. And to do that, we need love: *authentic* love, not a cheap replica. The "civilization of love" starts in the home.

Teach the habit of gratitude.
Despite all of our modern material advantages, we live in a joyless world. It's a world soaked in the message that we don't have enough things, that we need *more* things, that we *deserve* more things, and that we should get the things we want *right now*.

Strong families naturally refocus our hearts on gratitude, on being joyful with what we have—or, more precisely, with what God has given to us. Gratitude, as Dietrich Bonhoeffer once said, is the beginning of joy. And joy is worth seeking because, in the words of God's Son, "These things I have spoken to you, that

my joy may be in you, and that your joy may be full"
(Jn 15:11).

Create silence.

Romano Guardini, one of the great Catholic theologians
of the last century, described the value of silence this way:
"Only he who is able to be silent can speak meaningfully;
otherwise he talks nonsense. . . . To be capable of silence
is a virtue. He who does not know how to keep silence
does the same thing with his life as a man who would only
wish to exhale and not inhale. We need only to imagine
this to feel terrified. The man who is never silent dissipates
his humanity."[33]

The devil Screwtape described noise as the music of
hell. Parents might profitably check the levels of noise in
their homes, and in their own lives.

Finally: Pray together.

"The family that prays together, stays together." It's an old
adage, but also a true one. Prayer needs to be a central
activity of family life. Prayer binds the family together in a
common project of praise and thanksgiving, and the time
it involves seals the family bond. It's in prayer that a family's
hopes can be expressed, shared, and made fruitful by the
grace of God. Nothing can take its place.

Where does this leave us?

"The family," John Paul II wrote nearly thirty years
ago, "has always been considered as the first and basic
expression of man's *social nature*. . . . A truly sovereign and

spiritually vigorous nation is always made up of strong families who are aware of their vocation and mission in history." It's precisely because the ties of blood, kinship, and family bind us so tightly that humans will live and work *and, when needed, die* to have their families flourish. This explains why "the history of mankind, the history of salvation, passes by way of the family."

It also explains why, in the words of John Paul, "the Church considers serving the family to be one of her essential duties." Therefore, to the Church we now turn.

8

ECCLESIA SUA

"How do I typically think about the Church? Mother, when I receive the sacraments. Community, when I visit with, or work with, or I'm at Mass with fellow Catholics. I don't think of the Church as an institution. When I see the Church referred to as an institution, it's a red flag for me that the person is using the term to try to force a change in what she teaches."

A consecrated woman

"I think the crisis in the priesthood is due, in part, to a de-emphasis on the Church as spouse. A priest should understand his vocation as a husband, not as a functionary. It seems that when that [spousal] aspect of the Church is lost, the priesthood can attract men with significant sexual dysfunctions and issues relating to women. I would say that the use of the feminine personal pronoun 'she' in reference to the Church is essential."

A young priest

PEOPLE GIVE THEIR LIVES TO, AND FOR, ALL SORTS OF things. Some things are worthy. Some are not. Either way, as we've seen, where we focus our time and resources reveals what we treasure most. If we value a thing highly enough, we'll be willing to die for it. For many people throughout history and still to this day, the Church and the faith she teaches are, taken together, the greatest such precious thing. As I typed these words in the spring of 2020, Christians were dying by the hundreds in Nigeria at the hands of Islamist murderers. In China, North Korea, Vietnam, India, and much of the Islamic world, Catholics and other Christians endure harassment, discrimination, and violence simply because of their faith.

Christians are now the most widely persecuted religious group on the planet. In the United States, the willingness to die for one's faith is a matter of theory. Not so elsewhere. Christians in Africa and Asia deal with it as a tangible daily fact. Meanwhile, tens of millions of their fellow believers in Europe and the Americas seem blind to their suffering. This is partly due to the self-absorption encouraged by consumer economies. But the disinterest of most mainstream media compounds the problem.

Why such hatred and oppression? The reason is simple. Christianity, lived properly, is never a quiet presence in any society. It always has public implications. It competes for people's deepest loyalty by focusing the soul on the consequences of our actions not only in this life, but also for the next life. Thus, since apostolic times, the Christian faith has always been a personal experience, but never a merely private one. By its nature, the Gospel is missionary. Believers are charged to preach, teach, and convert the world, both as individuals and as a community.

As a result, Christians have always come together to

share and worship in the *ekklesia*, the Greek word (*ecclesia* in Latin) for those "called out" into public assembly. This is the source of our understanding of "Church." And it refers both to local church communities and to the one, holy, catholic, and apostolic Church of the Nicene Creed.

All Christians have some sense of belonging to a "church." But for Catholics, Church authority, tradition, and structure are especially robust. This gives the Catholic faith several great strengths. It has a powerful missionary focus. It has a long tradition of intellectual and cultural excellence, a heritage integrating faith, reason, beauty, and the arts. It has a real and vivid global unity. And with that unity comes the durability to survive extraordinary persecution. These same strengths, though, can also breed problems. The first is institutional sclerosis. The second is a kind of ecclesiolatry, or stressing the doctrines and offices of the Church in an unbalanced way, at the expense of immersing ourselves in God's Word and pursuing a relationship with Jesus himself.

Popes have spoken eloquently on the nature and importance of the Church.[1] In his 1943 encyclical *Mystici Corporis Christi* ("On the Mystical Body of Christ"), Pius XII described the Church as man's "only haven of salvation." For Pius, borrowing from St. Paul (Rom 12:4–5, Col 1:18, 1 Cor 12:13), the Church is a living organism of many members with different tasks. Together these members make up the one Body of Christ on mission in the world. And united with Jesus as the head, the body is fed by the Eucharist and sustained by all the sacraments.

Pius underlines the importance of pope and bishops, but he also stresses the vital role all members play in the life of the Church (nos. 40–44).

John XXIII, in his 1961 encyclical on social progress, highlighted the Church as *Mater et Magistra*, the "mother and teacher of all nations . . . [holding] the world in an embrace of love, that men, in every age, should find in her their own completeness in a higher order of living, and their ultimate salvation." For Pope John, the Church is the "pillar and ground of the truth," with Christianity "the meeting-point of earth and heaven . . . [laying] claim to the whole man, body and soul, intellect and will."

Finally, in the midst of the Second Vatican Council, Paul VI issued the 1964 encyclical *Ecclesiam Suam* ("On His Church"). Like John XXIII, he describes the Church as a loving mother. But he harks back especially to Pius XII's image of the Church and her members as the Body of Christ, the living presence of Jesus in human affairs.

Just three months after Paul's encyclical, the gathered council fathers built on Scripture, all these papal documents, and the long experience of the Christian community in offering the council's thoughts on the nature of the Church. The results were two key conciliar documents. The first, in 1964, was *Lumen Gentium* ("Light of the Nations"), the Dogmatic Constitution on the Church. The second, in 1965, was *Gaudium et Spes* ("Joy and Hope"), the Pastoral Constitution of the Church in the Modern World.

Lumen Gentium speaks *of* the Church as the "people of God," a sheepfold, and a spouse: the Bride of Jesus Christ. *Gaudium et Spes* speaks *for* the Church. It affirms the good in the modern world. It seeks to "enter into dialogue" about the world's problems. And it "offers to cooperate unreservedly with mankind in fostering a sense of brotherhood" to serve humanity's "noble destiny."

How these beautiful words have fared in the real world is worth pondering.

In 2016, the University of Pennsylvania released a report on the economic "halo effect" of the Archdiocese of Philadelphia, its ministries, and local Catholic entities.[2] It noted that the FY16 General Fund Budget of the City of Philadelphia was $4.0 billion. In comparison, the Archdiocese, its parishes, and its ministries contributed $4.2 billion *each year* to the local economy. Of that, diocesan-owned high schools alone generated nearly $250 million annually, not counting the long-term effects of the strong education they delivered.

The report projected the overall positive economic impact of the Catholic Church in the United States at $192 billion annually. It compared this with the *combined* FY14 state budgets of Delaware, New Jersey, Pennsylvania, and New York: $182.7 billion.

Put simply: The Church has always served the material needs of people, Catholic and otherwise, as part of her Gospel mission. She does this very well. The facts prove it. And her extraordinary witness is not diminished by the evil actions of various bad clergy and Church leaders. Her good vastly outweighs the bad—especially in a culture where sexual dysfunction, sin, and crime infect nearly every profession and public institution.

Increasingly, though, none of this matters. As political philosopher Patrick Deneen notes, many of America's cultural leaders have grown more and more hostile to any "carriers of tradition and morality that [are] viewed as obstacles to full realization of equal liberty," particularly in the realm of sex. And first in their gunsights is the Catholic Church.[3]

The social usefulness of the Church is thus a weak defense against hatred of her beliefs. The modern world that *Gaudium et Spes* spoke to so sincerely is often far more determined to convert the Church than to be converted *by* her. The City of Philadelphia, for example, was happy in 2018 to force the local Church into a long legal battle over foster care. The city's sole purpose was to coerce foster care services to refer children to homosexual couples; the proven quality of Church-related services and the gravity of religious conviction were irrelevant to the city's agenda. Tolerance, in today's sexualized political regime, tends to be a very narrow, one-way street.

Barring a cultural sea change, this will get worse. Christians in 2018–19 made up 65 percent of adult Americans. This was a 12 percent drop in one decade. At the same time, persons with no religious affiliation rose from 17 percent to 25 percent. Less than half of millennials claim to be Christian, and 40 percent are unaffiliated.[4]

The nation's religious roots, historically so influential in American public life, are drying up.

It doesn't take a think tank to see where this can lead. Constitutional protections exist on paper. But they're interpreted and applied by real persons on courts, and in elected and appointed positions of power. Religious freedom is only important to people who see faith as vital to the common good. Many of those people are aging out. It's no surprise, then, that legal challenges to religious liberty have spiked over the last few decades. That will continue.

American Catholics have gone through periods of prejudice and even occasional violence since the nation's founding. But overall, the United States has always been a good place for religious believers, including Catholics. In the future, that may not be so. The Church is only as strong as her core: the people fully committed to her and to her mission. As the number of active American Catholics declines, so will the material resources of the Church. This is already happening. The burden of sustaining the Church and her witness will shift more heavily onto those who remain: those willing to suffer the discomfort of believing and practicing truths seen as unwelcome by a changing nation. It won't be a pleasant experience. But it will be an honest one.

※

Two of my favorite saints are Thomas More, the layman, and John Fisher, the bishop. In life, they were friends. In death, they were martyred within weeks of each other, and for the same reason, by Henry VIII. Henry had broken with Rome. He claimed headship of the Church in England. They refused to cooperate. They were tried and convicted of treason in 1535. They gave their lives *precisely* for the Church.

Both men had been influential. More had been a leading attorney, philosopher, and statesman, finally serving as England's Lord Chancellor. Fisher had been chancellor of Cambridge University, a tutor of Henry VIII, and confessor and counselor to Lady Margaret, the king's mother. Both men had been highly esteemed at court before balking at Henry's split with the pope. Both men had a reforming spirit. Despite his privileges and the episcopal habits of his day, Fisher spent much of his time in his diocese of Rochester, then the poorest in England, serving its people. More died defending papal authority, despite his own deep misgivings about corruption in the Church and especially in Rome.

The layman and the priest: they were friends. Both loved the Church despite her many scars from sin. Both were willing to suffer for their faith despite the cost. And therein lies a lesson. This is how the Church not only survives but gives light to the nations: not through eloquent words, as important as they can be, but through the witness of her people, the prominent few and the many more unnamed faithful who love her. It occurred to me as I wrote this text that, in my fifty years as a priest, I'd met many such good persons; too many to count. So one evening I sat down and made a list of basic questions about the Church. Then I sent it to several dozen women and men, clergy, lay, and religious. Each person differed in personality and background. But all had moved me, over the decades, with their genuine faith.

Nearly everyone replied. Most answered every question. I offer some of the representative responses here, anonymous, candid, and only lightly edited for easier reading: laypersons first, since they comprise more than 90 percent of the Church; and then clergy. I'll offer my own thoughts as this chapter concludes.

From an attorney, wife, and mother: "*How do I think of the Church? Three ways: As a dysfunctional family, but MY family that will never break up but always come back together even after a fight. Also as a tribe of blood relatives, with built-in sympathy for each other, even before they actually meet. And finally as the most brilliant community in the history of the world. I love the Church; I love her because she is brilliant, and this delights me and leads me forward. God help me, but I love brilliance. And I thank God for this never-ending stream of brilliant women and men, on and on, century after century, gleaning more and more, expressing it this way and that, challenging what is incomplete or mistaken, revealing God, and accounting for the life I see in the world better than anyone who lacks a God-horizon.*"

From a leader in men's ministry, husband, and father: "*I see the Church as mother because she brings the living presence of God into my life. Every time I enter my home parish, the Church is Mary, inviting me to come near to the creche.*

For me, there's an overwhelming intimacy to the experience of the Church. At the same time, I think of her as an institution being run by very flawed human beings. Yet God somehow guides the whole embarrassing circus. The fact that we haven't managed to destroy ourselves as a Church is a very real sign of God's love for us."

From a consecrated woman: *"I see the Church as a mother who gave Christ to us; everything else about her flows from this, both community and institution. . . . I see and feel the Church as intimately connected to Christ, beautiful, perfect, and comforting. And she gives me such joy and hope. Then there's the institution that has evolved around her, and maybe since it's administered by human beings, it's flawed because we're so flawed. When I see selfishness, pride, greed, or outright criminal behavior, I remind myself that this is man's doing, not Christ's, and not the Church's."*

From a convert, husband, and father: *"What gives me the most joy about the Church? The Eucharist, without question. I'm not a huge Chesterton fan, but he was right that we need the Church to be right, when and where we're wrong. The Church needs to tell me about the parts of the Bible I wish weren't there, rather than say they aren't important. The Church gives me a home with spiritual peers I never had before and is more of a family than I ever experienced. Most of all, the Church gives us the sacraments, and they've allowed me to encounter Jesus with greater intimacy than I ever knew.*

"What troubles me the most about the Church? The shabbiness and mediocrity. And the corruption and scandals that go all the way to the top. After the summer of 2018, I didn't

want to baptize my newborn son. I didn't want to give him the Church as his family inheritance, and I didn't want to place him under the spiritual headship of knaves and fools. I never expected to feel that way as a Catholic, and I hope I never do again. What gives me the most hope? The number of holy priests and religious I know, and the fellowship of holy, joyful families."

From a longtime friend and businesswoman: *"What gives me the most joy about the Church? The love and charity of good priests. I've been blessed to experience this firsthand. I'll always remember and appreciate the funeral Mass for my son who was murdered. I'd been away from the Church for many years. But that pastor's charity brought me lasting peace. That simple, solitary act was the start of my journey back to Christ's Church. And I'll always remember the hospital chaplain who administered the sacraments to my Dad, prior to his 'routine' surgery. My father had been away from the Church for more than 40 years. As it happened, the surgery wasn't so routine. He never woke up."*

From a scholar, husband, and father: *"I tend to think of, and take comfort from, the Church as 'communio sanctorum,' the communion of saints extended across the ages with exemplars of truth, endurance, and grace. And I love her because, in spite of everything, she's the most beautiful thing in the world. What gives me joy is the Eucharist, of course, but also the sheer beauty of her traditions and patrimony. What gives me hope is young Catholics. What troubles me, on the other hand, is the loss of a real apprehension of God in the modern world, which manifests itself in the very heart of the*

Church as a loss of faith so profound that it doesn't see itself for what it is. Charles Péguy named it perfectly when he said that the problem with Christians is that they don't believe what they believe. This underlies the many crises that afflict the Church on the practical level: pervasive sexual problems, the obvious loss of confidence in theology and philosophy, the reduction of Christianity to politics, etc."

From a postgrad student, wife, and mother: "*We wanted to start our married life right in the heart of the Church. So we went to Rome for our honeymoon and brought our wedding clothes so that we could attend the Wednesday audience for the special 'Sposi Novelli' blessing and have our marriage blessed by Pope Benedict. At that time of my life, some nine years ago now, the Church felt very much like a mother who was nourishing our marriage with her sacramental grace. If we'd been married in the last few years, though, we would have skipped Rome and gone to Hawaii.*

"*I've stayed in the Church because of grace, particularly because of the Blessed Sacrament, but also because I was drawn to truth, the truth which the Church proclaims. I love the Church the way a daughter might love a mother who was once nourishing and kind and reasonable, but now suffers from dementia and is prone to being inattentive, irrational, and sometimes vindictive, attacking the things you care about; things you ironically care about because years ago she taught you to care about them. You ask what gives me joy? It's the good, holy priests in the everyday life of my family. Good men who are manly; who aren't weird or effeminate and who genuinely love Jesus Christ and are prepared to step up and*

*be real fathers, who take their prayer life seriously. There's
nothing better."*

From a veteran educator, husband, and father: "*I think
about the Church first as the Kingdom of God, with Jesus as
King and Lord. Then as the Body of Christ, because of the
Eucharist and the mystical reality that Christ taught Paul on
the road to Damascus ("why are you persecuting me?"). Then
as the Bride of Christ. Lastly as an institution. Why do I love
the Church? I love her for the sake of Jesus Christ, who loved
me and suffered to redeem me. Therefore I seek to serve him
by loving the Church.*

*"Was Vatican II naïve about the modern world? I grew
up with that bias and shared it for most of my adult life
before realizing it was wrong. 'Gaudium et Spes' is 'naïve'
not so much in its vision of the world, as in its lack of an honest critique of the Church. The council fathers did not take
up the more painful and difficult task of self-examination.
No reform of the world can effectively take place without
first a deep humility and interior conversion. Vatican II
was naïve not toward the world, but toward how worldly
the Church had become. What does it matter if we put the
liturgy in the vernacular (which is a good idea), if we speak
words of worship but our hearts are far from obeying God?
Aggiornamento—the Church's 'updating' and opening to
the world—eclipsed real reform. Aggiornamento doesn't
require the cross."*

From a retired journalist, wife, and mother: "*I don't
worry much about the bureaucracy of the institutional
Church, because Jesus will be with us in spite of anything*

the institution does or doesn't do. I rely first on Jesus Christ and take the institutional Church into consideration as long as she doesn't interfere with his teaching. I thank God that my faith was never grounded in the knuckleheads who run the Church, not that they're all knuckleheads, but we need to judge leaders by their actions. We need leaders who, like the Apostles, are not afraid to live and if necessary to die for the faith; to stand up for the teaching of the Church, not to punish those who do."

And finally, from a corporate consultant, husband, and father: *"What gives me joy in my life with the Church? Moments of redemption. I've seen how the experience of the Church leaves an indelible mark on the life of a person and forms an essential brace in the relationship between God and man. Our everyday 'tasks' as a Church change people's lives and create the spaces for them to meet the Lord. I've seen it. I've experienced it personally. We can miss God without the Church to slow us down, to point God out, to remind us of his presence. Observing and occasionally helping the Church create those spaces is what brings me so much joy."*

※

OVER THE YEARS, far more attention has been paid to Thomas More than to John Fisher. And that makes sense. More was a layman, a devoted husband and father. He had a rich domestic life. His friend, the great humanist Erasmus, wrote vividly of the warmth and humor of the More home. But, as many of the laypeople noted above confirm, the heart of Catholic life is the Eucharist. And there is no Eucharist without the priest. If we overlook John Fisher, we overlook a vital pillar of the Church: the men who feed the faithful with preaching and teaching, Scripture and sacrament.

John Fisher was a "priest's priest." He was a pastor of intelligence, zeal, and humility. He twice turned down transfer to much wealthier dioceses. In an age when absentee bishops were common, Fisher made comprehensive visitations to parishes throughout his diocese in 1505, 1508, 1511, 1514, 1517, 1520, and 1529. A biographer notes that he "was committed to the service of his people. . . . He spared no effort to meet the pastoral needs of his diocese, to provide the people with leadership and encouragement, and to protect them from error and confusion."[5]

Fisher worked hard to renew the study of theology. He had a passion for improving the preaching skills of his brother priests. And as for his character: early in his reign, Henry VIII praised Fisher for his "great and singular virtue [and] natural wisdom, and specially for his good and gracious living."[6] It's precisely Fisher's virtue that may have led a bitter and older Henry to desecrate the bishop's body after execution.

Holy priests, to borrow a thought from St. John Vianney, make holy laypeople. So it's worth hearing the responses of a few good priests to the questions I posed.

From an assistant pastor: "*How do I think about the Church? I remember sitting in the back pews of my seminary chapel. Once a week, the seminary would offer night prayer for any seminarians and evening lay students who wanted to attend. Often, I'd go down, tired after a long day, and not even bring my breviary. Instead, I would—and I was conscious of this after a while—let the Church carry me in prayer. That's what it felt like: the common experience of believers praying the ancient psalms supported me at those moments. In that sense, the Church is a mother who carries us in her arms. She's also a community of believers who support each other as Aaron and Hur held up Moses's arms in prayer. And by necessity, she's also an institution, one subject to human institutional dynamics, with both amusing and scandalous results. In those moments, at the end of a burdensome day, the Church, for me, also became like a spouse; one I could 'go home' to, one that drew forth from me new possibilities I didn't know I had in me, and that at the same time could be a great consolation."*

From a newly ordained priest: "*I love the Church not because she's easy to love, but because my faith became real within her bones. I love the Church because I love Jesus Christ, and like in any real marriage, it becomes impossible to separate the two. What God has made one, can never be undone.*

"*It's the intimate personal relationship with Jesus that drives a man into ministry in the Church. This always needs to be the priest's first and singular focus. The moment the Church becomes defined by her bureaucratic duties is the day those offices need to be destroyed. They're no longer supporting the mission to proclaim the Gospel. But if these same duties can truly serve the work of bringing people closer to Jesus, then they deserve their place. It's just not first place. Again, priestly ministry is like a marriage in which the spouse has real work obligations but also an intimate commitment to his or her family. Parents trick themselves if they think their work excuses a poor personal engagement with each member of the family. Exactly the same applies to a priest and his parish family."*

From a priest religious: "*I love the Church because she's the sacrament of salvation. I love the Church because of the riches she offers to the world, both despite and because of the world's persistent rejection of the sign that she is, the sign pointing toward Jesus Christ. I love the Church because of her people: I've had negative interactions with only a vanishingly small number of people I've met in the Church; the bond of unity that she can be at her best is amazing and invigorating. And I love the Church for reasons that I know will only become clear to me after years more of experience, the way that even in a marriage, one can learn something new about a spouse one loves.*"

From a student priest: "*The hardest thing for me about the current reality of the Church has been the weakness of her leadership. On every level, from parish leadership through the ranks, strong leadership in recent times has been lacking. What seems to have been sacrificed in the last few decades is an authentic understanding of the 'munus regendi'* [office of pastoral governance]. *In an effort to correct authoritarian styles in the past and to draw the laity more fully into the life of the Church, pastors have sacrificed what is properly theirs—the authority to govern and shepherd by virtue of their configuration to Christ the Shepherd. A stress on creating welcoming communities, which is obviously important, has eclipsed the need for courageous teaching and admonition. While the intentions may be very good, the truth is that weak leadership has harmed the life of the Church and needs correction."*

From a veteran priest and religious superior: "*You ask why we need the Church, especially since many good Christians seem to get along well with Scripture alone. I've asked the same question. I've asked myself whether the visible, hierarchical Church is really necessary for the Gospel. I conclude yes. First, I look at the Church's history, at the writings of the Fathers of the Church, and I'm convinced that it's the will of God that the Church exists with her structures and priesthood, with dioceses and bishops, and with a pope. The Church is apostolic, that is, the same Church through the centuries. Without the Church's structure, that would not be so. Read Ignatius of Antioch and Clement of Rome, two very early Fathers. For them the Church's hierarchical structure is essential. It's the Church's visibility (her hierarchy, dioceses, and structures) that assures that the Church is faithful to her apostolicity and her catholicity.*

"*Eastern Orthodoxy, I would argue, has devolved into utterly non-'catholic' (i.e., universal) entities. The Romanian Orthodox have no reason or ability to go to Indonesia to evangelize anyone, for example. Catholics and Protestants have a heart for evangelizing the whole world. But I believe that Protestant Christianity with all of its individual communities in a bare communion with one another, or in a communion based only on a Bible which is interpreted differently by every pastor, loses apostolicity and catholicity."*

From a pastor: "*Why is history, and especially Church history, important? History is humanity's greatest teacher. It's more than just a record of dates and dead people. It's the story of success, triumph, failure, and disappointment. I think Church history is the greatest testimony to divine grace, but very far from a story that's triumphant. It reminds mankind of our total failure to follow Christ, and the constant call we're given for renewal. In some ways, Church history is similar to how the Jewish people recount themselves in the Hebrew Scriptures. They often don't record their greatest stories but rather their worst. They show their humiliating attempt to follow God by underlining their failures and his fidelity. Church history is much the same. The story of the one true Church is marked by schism, sin, scandal, and suffering. And we need to learn from it.*"

From a priest based abroad: "*You ask what I think fidelity to Peter really means and requires. The specific role of the Pope is to be a sign and source of unity, to be an arbiter of conflict when necessary, and to clarify points of doctrine in an authentic development of the deposit of faith. When he exercises this office in continuity with the magisterial teaching which has preceded him and with due authority, the faithful need to give their assent. It does not mean that the Pope is a divine oracle free from personal error, whose word can never be challenged. Scripture attests to this with the example of Paul's admonition of Peter. Fidelity to Peter does not mean blind acceptance of, or undiscerning assent to, everything that a Pope says or does. The Pope enjoys supreme authority and a totally unique charism. But he remains part of the 'Christifideles.' He too is bound to the dogmatic and doctrinal proclamations of the Church that preceded him. He's not the inventor of doctrine but its guardian. If in any way a Pope were to seemingly violate these principles, it would not just be permitted to the faithful, but in fact the duty of the faithful, to challenge that violation."*

From a priest religious: "*Was Vatican II too optimistic? Yes. In speaking about technology, Peter Thiel likes to say we were promised flying cars, and instead we got Twitter and 140 characters. What happened in the Church after the council is a similar failure: We were promised an opening to the modern world that would be met with open arms, and what we got was churches, seminaries, and schools emptying out as we squandered our inheritance, leaving us with no resources to push back against the on-rushing of modernity that didn't need an opening on the part of the Church. It was coming anyway. Humans being what they are, and myself being a religious, I resist neat explanations of human behavior. But the council did seem to assume that somehow human nature had changed. There was no reason to think that was true, except that we had somehow managed not to kill everyone on the planet to that point. That's not evidence. It's luck.*"

From the pastor of a large parish: "*What gives me the most joy in the Church is seeing the power of the Gospel embraced and actually lived out in the lives of the People of God. And in watching the work of the Sacrament of Penance; how confession can bring a dead soul back to life through the movements of the Holy Spirit. The Church's teachings have an internal coherence and reasonability that I've always found deeply beautiful. And there are so many, many clergy and laypeople in my life that I admire and look to for friendship and leadership. There are a lot of people working hard, and often invisibly, for the good of the Church. Many of them are young, and that's a great cause for hope. Fundamentally though, hope resides in the fact that the Church belongs to Jesus Christ. She's his Church. And he will not abandon her."*

Two final observations; the first from an assistant pastor: *"We have a major problem with money. And it has very little to do with needing more money. Peter and John had neither silver nor gold. So why does the Church exist? Is it to keep people employed? To maintain a certain bureaucratic structure? In our need to keep up our operational budgets, we've created a fee-for-service model in many places. This wasn't done maliciously, at least in the vast majority of cases. But think about it: When parents bring their children to be baptized, they give some money to the priest. When funeral directors call a parish, one of the first questions is about the 'church fees.' Weddings feature a church fee, along with a stipend for musicians. When people come to Sunday Mass, they put their envelope in the basket. It can make one think that the Church is just another kind of entertainment entity. In business, the customer is always right. But the Church is not just another consumer organization. She's the*

Body of Christ. Any other perspective makes our salt lose its taste.

"*Yet in the face of all our problems, I find my smallness weirdly comforting. God doesn't need me at all. I'm just a speck of dust on a larger speck of dust. And still, for all that: God wants me. That's the only possible explanation for my existence: If he doesn't need me (and he doesn't), then he wants me to exist. And this gives me—and all of us—freedom. It means we should do what we can, and do it well. That's all he asks us to do. And because of this, the small, seemingly insignificant decisions we each make are actually what move history along, not the pretenses of the arrogant.*"

Second, from another student priest: "*I don't believe that Vatican II was overly optimistic; it was absolutely correct in its desire to present the Gospel in a manner more readily accessible to world of its day. But the results have been mixed. One of the things I would change if I could is the spirit of activism that now dominates so much of everyday Church life; a hyper-activity focused on doing, events, projects, celebrations, etc. These all have their place. But at times they seem to work against a contemplative spirit in the faithful, and to preclude environments conducive to contemplation. The human spirit can only truly ripen and mature by contemplating the deep things of the Spirit. This balance of contemplation and activity is modeled by Christ himself in the Gospels. Jesus would often steal away from the frenetic activity of ministry to immerse himself in the heart of his Father in contemplative prayer. It was this immersion in God that in turn gave life to Christ's continuing ministry. There's an urgent need today to recover this contemplative dimension if any real renewal in the Church is to be brought about."*

❧

AND SO WE come to the point where the author submits himself to some of the same questions he imposed on others. So now we'll turn to my own thoughts as a bishop, but more importantly, as a Christian believer in the Catholic Church.

How do you think of the Church—mother, spouse, community, institution? All four? Which most commonly?

I think of the Church as a mother more than anything else. Before being a priest or bishop, I was a baptized Christian, and my family taught me to love the Church from a very early age. She was never presented to me simply as an institution, but rather as the source of our spiritual life. Later, as a Franciscan, I was formed even more deeply in reverence for the Church. St. Francis thought it vital that all his friars be truly "Catholics." Many reform groups sprang up during Francis's life, and many of them were hostile to the Church. That's why Francis stressed the importance of being Catholic. In Francis's *Testament* a provision actually exists for prison rooms in friaries for friars who weren't truly Catholic. That tends to get missed in the modern "flower child" portrait of the saint. But on matters of fidelity to the Church and her teaching, Francis was a formidable man.

With Vatican II, we started to see the Church more as a community, rather than through the lens of canon law, which emphasized the Church as a perfect institution. After 1970, when I became a priest, and then especially when I became a bishop, I understood the Church more as a spouse.

One of the big differences between lay and clergy Catholic experience is that laypeople love the Church as a mother, and clergy love the Church as a spouse. Just as a layman gives his life to his wife and children, priests, through our ordination and offer of celibacy, give ourselves to the Church as our spouse. We live with her. We work for her. Every moment of the day we're in her embrace. That's why clergy are called "churchmen." All of us in the Church are equally called to love God and to love Jesus personally. But what's unique about the clergy is the way we love the Church as a spouse. Obviously, the Church has institutional realities. The similarity to marriage has limits. But, as in any marriage, we priests can be angry about some of the realities in our "spouse" and want to change them. And, as in any marriage, family, or community, the Church has institutional dimensions that we finally need to understand and accept.

One other point: It's important for priests, who have the task of shepherding the Church, to see the Church as a community, and to understand our essential but limited role within that community. Otherwise we give too much attention to ourselves. That's what clericalism is about, when we don't situate the sacrament of Holy Orders in the context of the sacrament of Baptism. So we need to remember all four of those dimensions of the Church as mother, spouse, community, and institution.

Why do you love her?

It's through the Church that I came to know Jesus Christ and the Christian life. Not only is the Church the transmitter of that information, the Church transmits that life itself through the sacraments, and through the lived embodiment of the Gospels by members of the Christian community. As the early Fathers of the Church said, if you love God as a father, you need to love the Church as your mother.

How do you separate her as an intimate personal presence in your life from the clutter of offices and bureaucratic duties that have filled so much of your ministry?

It hasn't been hard for me. I never saw those offices and bureaucracies as being very important. Robert Conquest, the poet and historian, once said that the simplest way to explain the behavior of any bureaucratic organization is to assume that it's controlled by a cabal of its enemies.[7] I wouldn't go that far, but you get the point. I see Church offices and org charts as necessary aspects of today's Church life, but not essential to who she is. I've certainly seen the underbelly of the Church as a bishop, and even prior to that, as a confessor. But nothing has ever made me doubt the truth of the Church.

Why do we need her? Many good Christians seem to get along quite well with just Scripture.

The Church preceded Scripture, not the other way

around. We need the Church in order to be faithful to the Word of God, which wasn't passed on to individuals but rather given to the believing community. To interpret Christian life as mainly a relationship between myself and the Scriptures ignores where Scripture came from. It also makes me an independent little pope, and that kind of autonomy is the primary sin of Adam and Eve. Salvation is a personal matter, but it's found and lived in community.

What are the hardest things for you to accept about the reality of the Church? What disappoints you the most?

The hardest thing is the sex abuse scandal because of the pain caused to victims and the damage done to the mission of the Church. And I'm troubled by the many people who really don't believe what the Church teaches but still claim to be Catholic. I mean those who try to change Catholic life to reflect their personal views, rather than admitting that they're no longer Catholics and finding a different community where their views are shared by others. This is especially true among theologians and academics who try to remake the Church in their own likeness. I've also been disappointed by the lack of courage from bishops who'd rather keep peace than proclaim the fullness of the Gospel, and by the ambition I've seen in the episcopate, which can lead bishops to be too coy, too careful, in order to avoid stirring up opposition to themselves personally. Prudence is a virtue, but it becomes a vice when it replaces courage on matters of principle.

What gives you the most joy?

People who are faithful to Jesus in tough circumstances. Parents of children with disabilities who love and support such children, and who welcome them as a gift from God. People who are faithful to the Church on sexual issues even when one of their children might embrace a life contrary to her teachings, or when it's hard to be faithful on matters like contraception. Priests and religious who take on demanding ministries with generous spirits. Another source of joy is the creativity I see in laypeople building new ministries, support groups, and movements. Or young seminarians who are idealistic and join the seminary despite all the problems in today's Church. Young women who enter religious communities that are generous and faithful to Church teaching. Immigrant groups that give the Church a glowing example of commitment to communal Christianity and who are faithful to Catholic teaching despite the temptations to materialism in the United States today.

Whom have you admired most—clergy and lay—in your ministry, and why?

Benedict XVI and John Paul II are at the top of the list. I'll stop there. The list is long, and I wouldn't want to accidentally leave anyone out.

Was Vatican II too optimistic about human beings and the modern world?

All of us were optimistic in those days because of a fresh opening by the Church to the world. That was a good thing. But people take good things to extremes, and that's what happened. I certainly don't blame Vatican II for our problems today. All Church documents need to be read in historical context, not just *Gaudium et Spes*. Considering the time and place in which the council documents were written, they're all products of the Holy Spirit helping the Church to proclaim the Gospel. Do I think things are worse today than they were in my first years as a Capuchin in the '60s and '70s'? Yes, I do, because of the overthrow of basic Christian culture regarding life and sexual issues, and because of the growing illusion of autonomy that results from great wealth. "Progress" without God is a very narrow kind of progress that can, and has, bitten us. And it will continue to do so because God made us for himself, and our hearts will be wild and restless without him.

You were a delegate to three synods. What unique things did each one teach you about the Church? How did they disappoint you? How did they encourage or gratify you?

The first synod I attended, back in 1997, focused on the Americas. I was one of the delegates directly appointed by Pope John Paul II. It was a great experience, my first real participation internationally in service to the universal Church. It was there that I met then archbishop Jorge Bergoglio, from Buenos Aires. He was an impressive man and made good contributions to the discussion. We sat near each other because we'd been appointed archbishops at about the same time. The synod led me to seek out a much closer relationship with the Churches in Mexico and Latin America, and with Latino Catholics in the United States.

The other two synods—in 2015, on the family, and in 2018, on young people and the faith—were very different. I was a delegate from the US Catholic bishops' conference and much more experienced, so I probably sensed the political dynamics of a synod more clearly.

I was very disappointed by what I saw as manipulation of the synods and their agendas by elements within and outside the Church. Instead of being occasions for an honest exchange of ideas, both synods were dominated by efforts to reengineer the direction of the Church. Synods should be places where people speak freely and are anxious to listen to others. But both were exercises of power rather than efforts to arrive honestly at a common position through listening and the inspiration of the Holy Spirit. Neither of those synods encouraged or gratified me. In fact, I was deeply scandalized by the political maneuvering that took place in both. The one on the family was a very important synod with some very sharp tensions. The one on youth lacked some important voices and seemed to miss many opportunities to say anything significant, or deal with the real issues of the Church in our time.

If you had the power to change certain things in the Church today, what would you do with it? What needs to change?

I'd do all I could to make the Church holier. But there's not much any one person can do about that, other than working on oneself. And, of course, encouraging others by word and example. The Church should pay less attention to voices in the world and more to the voice of Jesus Christ and the movements of the Holy Spirit. Concerns about "appearing" certain ways often keep the Church from being what Jesus wants the Church to be. I also wish women had a greater voice in the Church, and I'm happy to see women more involved today in Church administration and practical leadership. There are many ways to do that without compromising what the Church believes and teaches on the ordination of women.

How should we think about the role of the pope? What does fidelity to Peter really mean and require; and what does it not?

Ever since becoming a bishop I've thought that the Vatican too much resembles a Renaissance court. We should return to a simpler view of the papacy. The pope is pope because he's the bishop of Rome, and because of that, he needs to be personally active in that role in his own diocese. The pope also has universal primacy, and he has the gift of infallibility when formally adjudicating matters of faith and morals. That's an important part of his role in maintaining the unity of the Church. All this means we should love the pope and receive his leadership with a mature spirit of obedience. His having universal jurisdiction doesn't mean, however, that he's the personal pastor of everyone in the local Churches. He's the personal pastor of the people of the Diocese of Rome. The Lord didn't decide that Rome should be the model of how we live as a Church in all parts of the world. Fidelity to the pope means loving him, obeying him, respecting his leadership, and having confidence in his magisterial teaching.

Why is history—especially Church history—important?

Because it helps us see the things that are universal and essential, and the things that aren't: things that are time-related in terms of structures. The work of a "College of Cardinals" has always existed in some form, for example. We need a body, whatever its name, that elects the pope. But I don't think the College of Cardinals, in its modern incarnation, is needed for other things. We already have the college of bishops to do that.

Any other thoughts?

Yes. History is the work of remembering. John Fisher and Thomas More gave their lives for the Church—*died* for her, with great tranquility—not as cogs in a religious machine but as sons of a loving mother, a mother who had filled their lives with truth and meaning, purpose and light, and the intimacy of God. So two simple, final questions follow: Would we do the same, and why?

THE KING'S HIGHWAY

"Belief in eternity does not tear us away from the present, as we are sometimes told, to make us lost in dreams: it works just the other way around. It is rather by disregarding eternity that Christians have disregarded their times."

Henri de Lubac

AS A YOUNG BISHOP DECADES AGO, I SPENT HOURS READING anything I could about leadership. People deserve good leaders. Great leaders seem to be born with special skills, and are therefore rare. But most persons have at least some seeds of leadership in their character, seeds that need just a little courage, wisdom, desire, and self-mastery to grow.

A good leader knows his strengths and cultivates them. He also knows his weaknesses. He enlists and acknowledges good cooperators to achieve what he can't do alone. He also accepts the demands that leadership puts on him: protecting the people in his care, placing their needs above his own, guiding them, giving them reasons for hope, and speaking with honesty. Honesty is the most unwelcome quality in a leader when the news is bad. But it always ranks among the most respected virtues of leadership. Honesty is humanity's anchor to reality.

A thought experiment I found in those early years of reading has stayed with me.[1] It's simple. It goes like this: Imagine your own funeral. Imagine being present, but unseen. And then imagine listening to the attendees talk about you. Imagine what you would *want* people to say. Then compare to what they might *actually* say, based on the record of your life so far. It's a sobering exercise with a serious lesson: *Begin with the end in mind.* Lead with a clear and good goal. Live the same way, toward a good end that others will remember as worthy.

Two things are striking about this thought experiment. The first is its candor. Much of American life now seems bent on ignoring or delaying death, or pretending it away, or panicking when it intrudes itself brutally on the public consciousness, as it did with COVID-19. Reports claiming that people will soon live to 150 or even 1,000 years old, as implausible as that may sound, are more and more common.[2] But in fact, the maximum human lifespan hasn't changed greatly in recorded history.

With good luck and decent food, people in ancient cultures could, and did, live into their seventies and eighties (see Ps 90:10 and 2 Sm 19:34–35, for example). The vast majority didn't, of course, because of disease, war, bad nutrition, primitive medicine, and hard labor. People live longer today, especially in wealthy countries, because of improved access to more and better food, supportive technologies, and effective health care. Average American life expectancy, for example, increased from forty-seven years in 1900 to seventy-eight years in 2000.[3] But our maximum life span *as a species* has not drastically increased. Fantastic claims of impending longevity deserve, at the very least, a good dose of skepticism. As the great Jewish bioethicist Leon Kass has noted, they also warrant our asking *why* anyone would want to live another seventy or seven hundred years in this world, even under the best conditions.[4] Death, as we discussed in chapter 2, is a source of fear. We all instinctively cling to life. But it's also a source of completion and release. The sheer honesty of pondering one's death forces a person to consider what matters, to choose a path, to focus on the direction and meaning of his or her life, and to treat others accordingly.

There's a second striking thing about our thought experiment. It was used in a popular text for teaching corporate leadership. But its roots lie elsewhere: in religion. Reflecting on death and its implications, as we also saw earlier, is a Christian discipline with a very ancient pedigree. The Catholic tradition of contemplating the "four last things"—death, judgment, hell, and heaven—tracks back to apostolic times and the Early Church. We will die. We will be judged. These things can't be evaded. And we'll spend our eternity either with God in a state of joy, or without him in a state very different.[5]

The earliest Christians saw death as a river that must

be crossed in order to share eternal life with God. Jesus, through his own death and resurrection, provided the necessary path. Christ described himself—his *person*—as "the way, and the truth, and the life; no one comes to the Father but by me" (Jn 14:6). Thus, as noted in the Acts of the Apostles (e.g., 9:2), the earliest believers called themselves not "Christians" but "followers of the Way." It was "the Way" that Saul persecuted before his conversion. And it was "the Way," as an image, that profoundly shaped later Christian thought about life as a pilgrimage from this world to the next along the road of faith. As Augustine wrote in his *City of God*: "The heavenly city . . . is a pilgrim on earth, [and it] calls forth citizens from all peoples, and gathers together a pilgrim society of all languages."[6]

Words like "the Way" and "pilgrimage" imply a journey and a destination. Humans are creatures of place. We need the familiarity of settled homes. But we're also endlessly curious; our imagination draws us to the horizon. The road invites the restless heart to see what lies beyond the next hill. Thus the idea of "the road" has magnetic force. Throughout history, the road has been the artery of human adventure and social intercourse. Across the modern Mediterranean world, roads still exist that were built by Rome to carry her legions from Gaul to Syria and Palestine. Older still is the "royal road," mentioned in the Old Testament (Num 20:17, 21:22), that connected Egypt and Mesopotamia and enjoyed the zealous protection of local kings because of its importance.

The special status of a "royal road," borrowing on the sacred character of kingship itself in the ancient world, had similar versions throughout Europe. It left a lasting imprint on Western memory. This is why the road, and the stories it carries, so often figure in memorable literature. The list is long, from George Orwell's *The Road to Wigan Pier*, Jack Kerouac's *On the Road*, Cormac McCarthy's *The Road*, and Robert Frost's poem "The Road Not Taken" to Chaucer's *The Canterbury Tales*, Tolkien's Lord of the Rings trilogy, and even Dante's *Divine Comedy*. Two particular tales of the road concern us here.

The first ranks among the great legends of early Christianity. The Church of Domine Quo Vadis stands on the Via Appia Antica, one of the main ancient Roman thoroughfares. It marks the place where, according to tradition, St. Peter unexpectedly met Jesus long after the Lord's resurrection and ascension. Peter, fleeing Nero's fierce persecution of Christians in the city, asks, "*Domine, quo vadis?*"; "Lord, where are you going?" Jesus answers that he's going to Rome to be crucified again. As Jesus disappears, Peter grasps the meaning of the apparition: Peter's mission is to stay and serve the people in his care, despite the danger. He heads back to Rome and to his martyrdom. He turns back *toward* his death with a purpose, not away from it.

The second tale has been translated into two hundred languages and more widely read in the English-speaking world than any other book in history, barring the Bible. John Bunyan's *The Pilgrim's Progress*, published in 1678, is one of humanity's great religious allegories. The story is simple but profoundly rich. Christian is a man tormented by the knowledge of his own sins. He fears God's wrath against the evils of the land where he dwells, the City of Destruction. Desperate, he flees, carrying the burden of his sins as a weight on his back. He meets Evangelist, who leads him to a narrow gate and sets him on the pilgrim road to the Celestial City, home of Creation's great King and the place of salvation.

Along the way Christian is attacked by enemies, deceivers, fears, and temptations. He's undermined by his own weaknesses. But he persists, helped by virtuous companions and friends. As he travels on, he grows in strength and faith. And finally, through all his travails, he comes to the Country of Beulah, "whose air was very sweet and pleasant, the Way lying directly through it," with the Celestial City itself ablaze in gold and shining on the horizon.[7]

The journey is complete—save for one final obstacle. Between Christian and the City's gate runs a river. There's no bridge. There's no way around it. Christian and his companion, Hopeful, must go through it. The water is deep and swift. Christian, swallowed by the waves, wracked by doubt and fear and besieged by evil spirits with the memory of his past sins, starts to despair and sink. In his terror of death, Christian cries out, "for my sins [God] hath brought me into the snare, and hath left me!"[8] All is—or all seems to be—lost.

Death is the first of the "four last things." In the words

of Presbyterian scholar Carl Trueman, it's "the final enemy . . . death remains sovereign." We "might be able to fool ourselves, for a time, that [mortality] is a chess game we can win. But ultimately, death will checkmate us."[9] All the technology and medical advances in the world won't defeat it.

⚘

FEW COMMENTS IN recent memory have been misused more often and more vapidly than Pope Francis's off-the-cuff remark, "Who am I to judge?" The Gospel records Jesus as warning us to "judge not, that you be not judged. For with the judgment you pronounce, you will be judged, and the measure you give will be the measure you get" (Mt 7:1–3). For our own sake and the sake of those we're tempted to criticize, we should take Christ's words seriously. Only God knows another person's soul. Condemning people demeans their God-given dignity, and the task of a Christian, as St. Paul tells us, is to speak the truth in a manner ruled by love (Eph 4:15).

But we still do need to speak the truth. Thus, throughout Scripture, God, his prophets, his son Jesus, and Christ's apostles all pass judgment—again and again, and often harshly—on evil words, actions, and patterns of behavior.

A life in Jesus Christ requires mature moral reasoning. It involves constant judgments about good and evil, the right and the wrong paths. Our decisions and actions matter. They have consequences. In the words of Joseph

Ratzinger, the Christian "knows that he must answer [to God] for his actions, that he owes an account as a steward of what has been entrusted to him. . . . Nothing and no one empowers us to trivialize the tremendous seriousness involved in such knowledge."[10] It's precisely our account-ability that gives life its dignity. And this makes sense: In reality, for God to be "good," he must also be just, and justice *demands* judgment.

As we've seen, the fear of death is often tied to a dread of terminal disease and pain, the loss of everything we've built and everyone we've loved. But as we age, and unless we're very good at lying to ourselves, we also become more vividly aware of our sins, our failures, our mistakes, and the harm we've done to others; the scandal we've given stretching back across a lifetime. Without faith, this can be an unbearable burden. But even with faith, the thought of being judged after death by a just God—the second of the "four last things"—a God who knows us better than we know ourselves, can cause deep unease.

In the Catholic tradition, each of us will face both a particular judgment, at the moment of death, and a general judgment with all of humanity at the end of time. In both cases, nothing will be hidden. We'll have no room for evasions or alibis. Our imagination of the next life is shaped and limited by our senses and our language. But whatever we imagine, the reality will be both different and more, for better or worse. Perhaps the most sobering prospect is that we'll likely be our own toughest prosecuting attorneys. We'll bring the same sharp candor we showed in judging others to judging ourselves. We'll see with radical clarity who we really are and what we've become.

The most frightening thought about death is not that God, when we meet him face to face, will be a "hanging judge" with a ledger of our crimes. Jesus repeatedly describes God as a loving Father. And no such Father will allow the destruction of his child unless the child actively prevents him from averting it. If a soul has an ember of love and kindness left from its earthly sojourn, God will seek to breathe it back to life. So the really terrifying thought about the afterlife is not that God may damn us. It's that we may freely damn ourselves. We may *choose* hell because we've made ourselves into the kind of creatures who prefer it.

Theologians have written great volumes on divine judgment. But for the everyday believer, C. S. Lewis may have captured the nature of God's justice and mercy best in his fiction. In *The Great Divorce*, lost souls are free to take a bus ride from hell to the threshold of heaven. But most, even on the brink of eternal bliss, are so jealously wedded to their sins that they refuse to discard them. Thus they cannot enter paradise. Even more powerful, for me, are the concluding chapters of Lewis's *The Last Battle*, the final book in the Chronicles of Narnia. *The Last Battle* recounts the apocalyptic end of the Narnian world, and the Last Judgment of its creatures by the Christ-figure lion, Aslan, at the great Door to heaven:

> The creatures came rushing on, their eyes brighter and brighter as they drew nearer and nearer. . . . But

as they came right up to Aslan, one or other of two
things happened. They all looked straight in his face; I
don't think they had any choice about that. And when
some looked, the expression on their faces changed
terribly—it was fear and hatred [and turning away,
they] disappeared in his huge black shadow. The
children never saw them again. I don't know what
became of them. But the others looked on the face
of Aslan and loved him, though some of them were
frightened at the same time. And all these came in at
the Door, on Aslan's right.[11]

Counted unexpectedly among the saved is a young
pagan prince. Though he served a false god and believed
himself to be an enemy of Aslan, he did so with a pure
heart, an innocent ignorance, and a passion for truth.
Aslan, in his mercy, accepts the prince's virtue and longing
for the truth as a search for, and a service to, himself—the
grounding of all truth.

Missing from Lewis's thoughts about God's judgment,
of course, is purgatory. As a Christian, though not a Catholic, he did at least acknowledge its plausibility. Lewis
described the idea of purgatory, should it exist, as a kind
of stinging mouthwash after the extraction of a bad tooth,
or as a beggar in rags, invited to a wonderful feast, might
accept the kindness of his host but ask for time to bathe
first and clothe himself appropriately. These are ingenious
approximations of what an afterlife purgation might be
like. But they're not finally satisfying. Perhaps a richer

portrait of what a purgatory might be like can be found in the short story "Leaf by Niggle," by Lewis's Catholic friend, J. R. R. Tolkien. But it too is incomplete.

One of the great ironies of the various sixteenth-century reformations was the unintended effect of attempts to cleanse Christian faith of "superstition." In stripping away relics, sacraments, veneration of Mary and the saints, indulgences, Masses and prayers for the dead, and—notably—purgatory, the more radical reformers fractured the Christian *communio sanctorum* ("communion of saints"): the intimate ties to one another of the Church Militant on earth, the Church Suffering in purgatory, and the Church Triumphant in heaven. The living links between this world and the next disappeared. As a result, for many, Christianity took on a strongly practical, this-worldly focus. Combined with decades of bloody religious conflict, this arguably set the stage for a decline in a sense of the supernatural, and the rise of modern secularism and unbelief.[12]

The Catholic faith holds to its belief in purgatory for sound reasons. God is utterly alien to sin. Grave evil ("mortal" sin) destroys a man's relationship with God. Lesser acts of evil ("venial" sin) mar and weaken the relationship, but they do not break it. Even a good person, a person sincerely committed to God, sins daily and carries the residue of those sins into his or her particular judgment by God at death. Justice demands their resolution. As the great German theologian, Romano Guardini, said, "God is almighty, but not a magician. . . . He does not render undone what has been done." We're forgiven our sins because of Christ's redemptive act. But, as Guardini argues, his righteousness cannot simply be hung about us like a concealing cloak. It needs to become part of our very selves. Thus, when a good man dies and enters into God's light,

> he sees himself as God sees him. He loves God's holi-ness and hates himself because he contradicts it. He feels his condition fully . . . and the experience must be one of inconceivable pain. But his suffering is effec-tive. His intention clarifies and expands until it reaches the fullness of good will. . . . It acts upon his being until the man not only desires to be good, but until goodness has become the form of his reality. In this process of becoming, dying and living again are bound up in a wonderful, terrifying mystery. A dying is con-tinually suffered out of which the new life springs.[13]

As Guardini stressed, "The dead in the hand of God do not, as such, call for pity. They are undergoing inconceiv-able suffering, but suffering that inspires awe," because "they suffer in expectation of their triumphant entry into glory." Our task is to remember them, to pray and have Masses offered for them—something too often forgotten today—and to ask their prayers in return for our own jour-ney toward God. As Dante wrote in the *Divine Comedy*, the souls ascending the Mountain of Purgatory are blessed by the certainty of their destination. They're simply ahead of us on the pilgrim's road.

❧

In 1967, near the height of his celebrity, the actor Richard Burton made an odd little movie. The film, *Doctor Faustus*, was based on Christopher Marlowe's play from the sixteenth century, *The Tragical History of Doctor Faustus*. Burton had a personal passion for this play. He acted in the film's lead role; he also served as codirector and coproducer. Derided by critics at the time, the production is largely forgotten today. But despite its many flaws, the film has aged better than anyone might expect. It's a great story in the hands of a great talent.

The plot is simple. The proud German scholar Faustus lusts for immense knowledge. Dissatisfied with human learning, he turns to magic, and from there, to dealing with the devil. He sells his soul to Lucifer, and in return receives twenty-four years of slavery to his every desire by Mephistopheles, one of hell's fallen angels. The pact is sealed. The devil keeps his bargain. But Faustus squanders his time on foolish stunts, tricks, and empty displays of power. In the end, paralyzed by despair, hounded by his sins, and unable to seek forgiveness, he's damned. In the play and in the movie, Faustus is dragged off to hell. But hell's most frightening description comes not at the film's (and original play's) end, but in the earliest exchange between Faustus and Mephistopheles:

Faustus: *Where are you damn'd?*
Mephistopheles: *In hell.*

Faustus: *How comes it, then, that thou art out of hell?*

Mephistopheles: *Why, this is hell, nor am I out of it:*
Think'st thou that I, who saw the face of God,
And tasted the eternal joys of heaven,
Am not tormented with ten thousand hells,
In being depriv'd of everlasting bliss?
O, Faustus, leave these frivolous demands,
Which strike a terror to my fainting soul.

A century later, in 1674, John Milton captured the same unnerving reality of hell in his poem *Paradise Lost*. In the space between his failed rebellion against God and his temptation of Adam and Eve, Satan wavers briefly in his wickedness:

Which way I fly is Hell; myself am Hell;
And, in the lowest deep, a lower deep
Still threatening to devour me opens wide,
To which the Hell I suffer seems a Heaven.
O, then, at last relent: Is there no place
Left for repentance, none for pardon left?
None left but by submission; and that word
Disdain forbids me.

Myself am hell, and Satan cannot escape it, any more than he can escape the poisonous self that his sin of pride has led him to become.

Hell, to put it mildly, is the least popular of the "four last things" to ponder. For the modern mind shaped by

scientism and its assumptions, the idea of eternal punishment is both cruel and implausible. To the nonbeliever,
the prospect of damnation can seem little more than a
religious means of social control and scaring people into
obedience. Thus the objections to hell will be familiar:
The devil is a premodern myth made ridiculous by psychology. No one can take seriously an afterlife with lakes
of fire and dragon-like demons. How can a loving God
sentence finite beings to infinite suffering? Even if such a
God *were* to exist, he'd be worth hating. And so on.

Answering these claims isn't hard. But convincing
people who'd rather not think too deeply, or who simply
exclude the afterlife as ridiculous in principle, *is*. The idea
that the envelope of our senses which we inhabit in this
world exhausts reality is not "rational." It's delusional, a
form of self-imposed blindness. The part of reality that
Christians call supernatural or spiritual is, at the very least,
plausible. Confidence in such a larger reality is nearly universal in human experience. Nothing in Christian belief
limits Satan to a leathery red demon with a pitchfork,
or hell to a boiling cauldron of torment. The images we
take from popular art and even Scripture are merely that:
images; suggestions of the reality.

What Christians *do* believe is that the Evil One is real,
a great but malignant personal spirit. As a rebel against
God, he's also the enemy of humanity. Romano Guardini
stresses that Satan is no mere metaphor, "no principle, no
elementary power, but a rebellious, fallen creature who
frantically attempts to set up a kingdom of appearances and

disorder . . . [who] attempts to tear the world from God's hands—even to dethrone God."[14] In discussing Christ's encounter with Satan in the desert, Joseph Ratzinger adds that the devil is also a gifted theologian, "a connoisseur of the Bible who knows how to quote the Psalm exactly; the whole conversation of the second temptation takes the form of a dispute between two Scripture scholars."[15]

As for the reality of hell: C. S. Lewis argued that "we know much more about heaven than hell, for heaven is the home of humanity and therefore contains all that is implied in a glorified human life: but hell was not made for men. It is in no sense *parallel* to heaven: it is the 'darkness outside,' the outer rim where being fades away to nonentity."[16] Whatever else it might be, hell is the permanent separation of a soul from its intended communion with God, who is love itself. "To enter heaven," wrote Lewis, "is to become more human than you ever succeeded in being [while on] earth. To enter hell is to be banished from humanity. What is cast (or casts itself) into hell is not a man: it is 'remains' . . . a will utterly centered in itself and passions utterly uncontrolled by the will."

Over the centuries, various Christian scholars have suggested that hell might exist but be empty of human souls, or that in the end all creatures, including Satan himself, might be saved. But this has never been the belief of the Church. We become what we choose and do. If we're truly free—and our faith teaches that we are, and that our dignity depends on that freedom—then we're free to choose badly, to choose against God.

Some will argue that hell offends God's mercy. So indeed it does. But again, if we're truly free, God cannot impose his mercy. The need for it must be admitted by the sinner, and then accepted. This requires humility. Humility requires honesty about the self and a submission of the will. Yet these are precisely the things that the damned have rendered themselves incapable of. Canceling the sins of the willfully selfish and unrepentant is not mercy but injustice. It erases any meaningful difference between wickedness and virtue. As to how expressions like "eternal death" and "punishment forever" might translate into experience: In the afterlife, words that imply an endless succession of days disappear into the unknowable. Time as we now understand it will no longer apply. What we do know is that hell, whatever its form, would be indescribably bad. How bad, we never want to find out.

One of the telling paradoxes of our age is that the more we've dismissed the existence of hell, the better we've become at building its replicas here on earth. Reflecting on sin and its consequences, and the reality of Satan and hell, is a good exercise in sanity. It's medicine for the spirit. If we live and die only for ourselves, we squander our time and gifts and deserve no better than Faustus. But it's also true that dwelling too much on the dark rim of the afterlife is unhealthy. Nor, since Golgotha, is it warranted. As a friend likes to say, Satan is the greatest tactician and worst strategist in the history of God's creation. He's fighting a war that he's already lost. He's powerless against Jesus Christ and Christ's own. And that knowledge feeds both his fury and his despair. Which leads to one final lesson about the Evil One.

Midway in his journey to the Celestial City, Christian of *The Pilgrim's Progress* finds his path blocked by Apollyon, a fearsome devil. Apollyon tries to humiliate, tempt, and cajole him, then bully and threaten him, into turning back. Christian stays firm in his purpose. The devil then breaks into "a grievous Rage." When Christian responds, "Apollyon, beware what you do, for I am in the King's highway, the Way of Holiness," the devil savagely assaults him. The struggle goes on for hours. No quarter is called or given. No help arrives. But in the end, defending himself with the shield and sword of faith, Christian pierces Apollyon, who flees.

The moral of the story is simple. God does not abandon us. He gives us the weapons we need for the road home. But the choice to go forward in faith or turn back in fatigue or fear: that's ours. It belongs to each of us alone.

※

HEAVEN IS THE last of the "four last things." It's also the worthiest goal to live and die for. It's the journey's end and ultimate purpose of every Christian pilgrim. But it's oddly difficult to talk about in a convincing way. A friend of mine, a wife and mother of many years, offered a reason. Most of us are keenly aware of our mistakes, failures, and sins, even if we hide them well. Imperfection is familiar. It's an intimate part of our lives. Perfection is the opposite. We yearn for it, but it's always just out of reach. How can anyone describe, or even fully understand, the meaning of a word like "bliss"? This is why so many of us find it easier and more vivid to imagine hell rather than paradise. The common mental portrait of heaven—singing in a choir on a cloud forever—sounds colossally tedious.

Of course, the *real* heaven, like the sparkle in a lover's eyes, or the warmth and adventure of true friendship, will have nothing about it tedious or static or routine. One of my favorite popular images of the afterlife is a banquet room that's identical in both heaven and hell, with the same spectacular meal and the same abnormally long utensils. In heaven, the souls feed each other and feast. In hell, they insist on feeding themselves, and starve. Love is unselfish and dynamic; it gives itself away. By its nature, it creates and expands. It makes all things new. And heaven will be the home of love, pulsing from the heart of God himself: an endless exhilaration of giving ourselves away, and receiving infinitely more in return.

There's a moment worth noting here in "A Short Story of the Anti-Christ," by the great Russian Christian writer Vladimir Solovyov. In imagining the Anti-Christ, Solovyov cast him as an exceptional man whose "clear intellect always showed him the truth of what one should believe in: the good, God, and the Messiah. In these he *believed*, but he *loved* only *himself*. He believed in God, but in the depths of his soul, he involuntarily and unconsciously loved only himself" (emphasis in original).[17] Like Solovyov's Anti-Christ, the devils too believe in God, but they hate him, because he renders their self-love empty and pathetic.

Perhaps this explains why C. S. Lewis said that heaven is "an acquired taste." The selfish soul may be incapable of choosing, enjoying, or even recognizing heaven. God made us profoundly social creatures. We're meant for mutual aid and encouragement, and these things hint at the nature of paradise. Heaven will be a personal affair, but not a private one. Learning to love God more than our own desires and appetites—and others because they're loved *by* God—is the substance of a Christian life. It demands the kind of honest self-examination that helps us weed out the self-love we hide so skillfully even from ourselves. This is why habits of prayer, the sacraments, and the silence needed for contemplation are so vital. They reshape us in a way that will "fit" in heaven.

"Loving God" sounds all very good and pious. But a sensible critic will note the obvious: it's a great deal easier to love someone we can see than someone we can't. If God is so lovable, why doesn't he show himself? Why does he hide himself (assuming he's really there)?

The short answer is also the best one: He *doesn't* hide himself. And he *does* show himself. Jesus of Nazareth is the face of God, God incarnate, his Word made flesh and blood. God knows us not merely as his creatures, animated pieces of his modeling clay, but also *from the inside*, as one of us. He knows our joys, fears, hopes, sorrows, and temptations not through some divine microscope but from direct human experience. Thus if we're really serious about seeing God, we simply need to look for him: he remains with us, and walks with us, every day in Scripture and the Eucharist.

He also reveals himself in the beauty of the world, and our instinctive need for it. As the philosopher Roger Scruton wrote, beauty hints at the divine. It's fundamental to human fulfillment. Man's desire for beauty "is a need arising from our metaphysical condition. [Beings] like us become at home in the world only by acknowledging our 'fallen' condition. . . . Hence the experience of beauty points us beyond this world to a 'kingdom of ends' in which our immortal longings and our desire for perfection are finally answered."[18]

Scruton spoke as a secular scholar. But he merely echoes St. Augustine, as quoted in the *Catechism*:

> Question the beauty of the earth, question the beauty of the sea, question the beauty of the air distending and diffusing itself, question the beauty of the sky . . . question all these realities. All respond: "See, we are beautiful." Their beauty is a profession. These beauties are subject to change. Who made them if not the Beautiful One, who is not subject to change?[19]

One other thought is worth mentioning. The Letter to the Hebrews notes that "It is a fearful thing to fall into the hands of the living God" (10:31). In context, the letter's author is focused on the gravity of God's judgment against those persons who, having received the truth, then repudiate or ignore it. But "fear of the Lord"—reverence and awe for God's majesty—is a theme throughout Scripture, and one of the gifts of the Holy Spirit.

Words like "wonder" and "awe" tend to lose their meaning in cultures dominated by scientism. But we dispense with awe for God's work and the mystery of the divine at our peril. The God of Jesus Christ is intimate and personal. Jesus asks us to call God "Abba," father. God is, in the final words of Dante's *Paradiso*, "the Love that moves the sun and the other stars." But he is also radically holy, transcendently Other, the God of justice and thunder as well as mercy, infinite power as well as love. In Moses's meetings with God on Sinai, God showed him only his "back," not his "face," so that his creature might continue to live (Ex 33:20–23). After the encounters, Moses's own face shined in a manner so drastically transformed that it frightened the Israelites, and he subsequently wore a veil (Ex 34:29–35).

Even in this world, in everyday life, events can sometimes be so exhilarating, so surprising, so intensely good, that they stun the senses and steal breath from the body. The joy of the Beatific Vision, an eternity in the overwhelming beauty of God's loving face, would be the *essence* of what Lewis called an "acquired taste," a taste only acquired through God's redemption and grace and a lifetime spent cooperating with both.

At this point, alert readers will recall that earlier in

these reflections we left Christian, John Bunyan's pilgrim, drowning in the river of death. We'll return to him shortly. In the meantime, though, before our final chapter, we'll close with one last item for thought.

The English poet and Catholic mystic Francis Thompson struggled with poverty, illness, homelessness, thoughts of suicide, and opium addiction throughout much of his life. He nonetheless wrote "The Hound of Heaven," one of the great religious poems of the last two hundred years. In Thompson's poem, the soul flees desperately from God. But God pursues, relentlessly, a tireless hound:

> I FLED Him, down the nights and down the days;
>   I fled Him, down the arches of the years;
> I fled Him, down the labyrinthine ways
>   Of my own mind; and in the mist of tears
> I hid from Him, and under running laughter.
>   Up vistaed hopes I sped;
>   And shot, precipitated,
> Adown Titanic glooms of chasmèd fears,
>   From those strong Feet that followed, followed after.
>   But with unhurrying chase,
>   And unperturbèd pace,
> Deliberate speed, majestic instancy,
>   They beat—and a Voice beat
>   More instant than the Feet—
> 'All things betray thee, who betrayest Me.'

And toward the poem's end, God speaks:

How little worthy of any love thou art!
Whom wilt thou find to love ignoble thee,
  Save Me, save only Me?
All which I took from thee I did but take,
 Not for thy harms,
But just that thou might'st seek it in My arms.
  All which thy child's mistake
Fancies as lost, I have stored for thee at home:
  Rise, clasp My hand, and come!'

Heaven is real. And if we do not pursue God, he will pursue us. We can elude him. We can refuse him. But until the last beat of our heart, the hound will keep following.

ON FRIENDSHIP

"Among all worldly things nothing seems worthy to be preferred to friendship. Friendship unites good men and preserves and promotes virtue. . . . It brings with it the greatest delight, to such an extent that all that pleases is changed to weariness when friends are absent, and all difficult things are made easy and as nothing by love."

Aquinas

"There is no greater consolation than the unfeigned loyalty and mutual affection of good and true friends."

Augustine

WHEN WE LAST SAW CHRISTIAN, THE GOOD PILGRIM IN John Bunyan's *The Pilgrim's Progress*, he was drowning in the river of death. Within sight of the Celestial City's gate, he was dragged down by fear and assailed by the memory of his sins. But of course the story doesn't end there. Throughout his journey, the Pilgrim has been aided by companions, helpers, and friends. And so it is at journey's end. His final friend, Hopeful—with him in the worst of the raging torrent—urges him on, reminds him of God's mercy and love, and helps him at last to the safety of life's far shore.

In Christian thought, the theological virtues—faith, hope, and charity—have a logical architecture. Faith is the foundation of a Godly life. We believe, and if our faith is sincere and deep enough, it allows us to trust. Trust involves risks. Faith supports the "weight" of trust and enables a life of hope. And that virtue of hope frees us from fear and allows us to forget ourselves. It enables us to love others with *agape*, the unselfish charity-love that seeks the best for others, even those who despise us, no matter what the cost to ourselves, while expecting nothing in return.

The theological virtues are gifts from God. We receive them as individuals. But they're sustained in community. As virtues, they survive and thrive with the help of others. Bunyan's Pilgrim perseveres on the brink of despair not because of his own strength but through the presence and encouragement of his friend. Curiously though, *philia*—the Greek word for friendship-love—has an ambiguous place in Christian thought. As the distinguished Lutheran scholar Gilbert Meilaender wrote some years ago,

> There can be little doubt that friendship was a considerably more important topic in the life and thought of the classical civilizations of Greece and Rome than it has, for the most part, been within Christendom.

With the possible exception of the literature of monasticism, friendship has never been a central concern of Christian thought. . . . Within Christian thought, *agape* displaced *philia*, and it is impossible to think theologically about love without giving that fact careful consideration.[1]

Meilaender notes five reasons for this seeming displacement.

First, philia is a preferential bond with a friend. The *agape* of the Gospel is non-preferential, like the love of God himself. *Second, philia* involves a mutual bond of freely exchanged love. *Agape* is given even to an enemy, with no expectation of reciprocal goodwill. *Third, philia* can degrade and disappear; human friendships can cool as the circumstances of life change. But *agape* should be marked by the same enduring fidelity that God shows to his covenant. *Fourth, philia* "was the noblest thing in the world in an age when 'civic friendship' was a widely shared ideal." Christianity, in its practical effect, desacralized politics, distinguishing the City of God from the City of Man, with the heart's search for a resting place in a God beyond this world. *Fifth, philia* was "the preeminent bond in a world for which work was of relatively little personal significance" beyond the obvious task of survival. But "*agape* helped shape a world in which vocation was seen as a supremely important form of service to the neighbor."[2]

The Greco-Roman world did, in fact, place a very high value on friendship. Aristotle dedicated two of the ten books in his *Nicomachean Ethics* to the subject of friendship. Cicero explored the same theme in his text *De Amicitia* ("On Friendship"). For Aristotle, friendship "is a sort of virtue, or at least implies virtue, and is, moreover, most necessary to our life. For no one would care to live without friends, though he had all other things."

He describes friendship as indispensable, beautiful, and noble. He goes on to stress that

> In poverty and all other misfortunes . . . we regard our friends as our only refuge. We need friends when we are young to keep us from error, when we get old to tend upon us and to carry out those plans which we have not strength to execute ourselves, and in the prime of life to help us in noble deeds—"two together" [as Homer says]; for thus we are more efficient both in thought and in action.[3]

True friendship, for Aristotle, is more than mere mutual utility, though friends naturally seek to help and be useful to one another when the need arises. True friendship is also more than the joy friends take in each other's company, though the pleasure of "fitting together" obviously animates friends. And true friendship is also more than a disposition of friendliness. We can be friendly with many people; we can be true friends with only a few. Friendship demands the investment of a person's time and energy. It involves risk, and also candor. It requires a willingness to place the task of loving the friend above our own natural appetite for being loved.

The true and highest form of friendship, for Aristotle, is that of good persons who resemble and reinforce each other in virtue. And the reason is simple. The friendship of good persons "grows with their intercourse, and they seem to become better as they exercise their faculties and correct each other's deficiencies, for each molds himself to the likeness of that which he approves in the other."[4]

We can find a bridge between Meilaender's observations and the ancient view of friendship in the work of C. S. Lewis.

In *The Four Loves*, Lewis notes that the modern world will gladly admit a person's need for a few friends. But in practice, *philia* as a distinct form of love is often seen as "something quite marginal; not a main course in life's banquet; a diversion." Friendship is the least "natural" of the loves; the least organic; and today, when social media can create a circle of virtual "friends" a mile wide and an inch deep, it's also the least richly experienced. We can live and breed without friendship, Lewis noted. Thus "the species," he wrote, "biologically considered, has no need of it. The pack or herd—the community—may even dislike and distrust it. Its leaders very often do." Friendship can be suspect because it occurs between and among private individuals, and "the moment two men are friends, they have in some degree drawn apart together from the herd."[5]

Lewis writes that

> We picture lovers face to face but Friends side by side;
> their eyes look ahead. This is why [people] who simply
> "want friends" can never make any. The very condition
> of having Friends is that we should want something
> else besides Friends. Where the truthful answer to the
> question *Do you see the same truth?* would be "I see
> nothing, and I don't care about truth; I only want a
> Friend," no Friendship can arise. . . . There would be
> nothing for the Friendship to be *about*; and Friendship
> must be about something.

Do you see the same truth? Or at least, do you *care about*
the same truth? For Lewis, these questions are ultimately
at the heart of every enduring friendship. Friends may
or may not agree on all the details, but what binds true
friends together, beyond pleasure and utility, is a common
quest or vision. Thus, he notes, "you will not find the warrior, the poet, the philosopher, or the Christian by staring
in his eyes as if he were your mistress: better fight beside
him, read with him, argue with him, pray with him."

For Christians, learning to love as God loves, with
purely selfless *agape*, will always be our goal. But as we
travel the King's highway and pilgrim's road, *philia*, the
love we share with true friends, is a special gift. It makes
life rich and the path less wearisome. As Lewis noted,
"Friendship is not a reward for *our* discrimination and
good taste in finding one another out. It is the instrument

by which God reveals to each the beauties of all the others. . . . At this feast [of friendship], it is *He* who has spread the board, and it is *He* who has chosen the guests" (emphasis added).

The image of friendship as a feast means that the guest list can make for some interesting memories. Lewis was brought to the Christian faith through his friendships with J. R. R. Tolkien and Hugo Dyson. All three played prominent roles in the loose, scholarly fellowship at Oxford University known to history as the Inklings. A mark of true friendship is candor, and Inkling discussions over brandy and meals could be lengthy and vigorous—and heated. Tolkien famously disliked Lewis's Chronicles of Narnia tales and wasn't quiet about it. He also famously dominated some of the Inklings' meetings by reading from his endless drafts of the Lord of the Rings novels.

Thus it was an exasperated Hugo Dyson, the Tolkien friend, committed Christian, and distinguished Shakespeare scholar, who finally, and famously, blurted out, "Oh no, not another [expletive] elf!"[6]

THE WORD "FRIEND" in English derives from Old English and Germanic words with the Indo-European root meaning "to love." The Old English word *freondscipe* translates as "mutual regard or liking." It can also mean "conjugal love." But it's only the perversity of our age, C. S. Lewis said, that sees an erotic subtext in every close friendship between two men or two women. In exaggerating the importance of *eros*, modern culture not only ruins *eros* by vulgarizing its beauty and rendering it just another, if pleasant, bodily function. It also degrades and impoverishes every other form of love.

If a marriage is to endure and bear its best fruit, for example, much more than *eros* is needed. Sexual desire can grow and fade and grow again, but its framework over time must be grounded in a deeper *philia*. All great marriages are first and finally friendships.

For the Christian, all of Creation expresses God's love. Scripture is one long and complicated but finally triumphant love story between God and his people. Genesis tells us that God walked as an intimate friend with Adam and Eve in the Garden before the Fall. And stories of friendship fill the Old Testament. In the book of Ruth, for example, Naomi and her husband leave Bethlehem and settle in Moab because of a famine. They have two sons. Naomi's husband eventually dies. Her sons, now grown, marry two good Moabite women, Opah and Ruth. But her sons soon also die. All three women are left as widows.

Naomi decides to return to Bethlehem. She loves her daughters-in-law. For their own sakes, she urges them to return to their Moabite blood relatives. Opah does so, but Ruth will not abandon Naomi. Faithful to her mother-in-law, she travels with her back to Israel. In Bethlehem, Ruth supports Naomi by laboring in the fields as a gleaner. She collects the scraps left behind by the harvesters.

The fields belong to Boaz, a kinsman of Naomi. Boaz admires Ruth's beauty and diligence. But above all, he reveres her fidelity to Naomi. He protects Ruth and provides for her. Seeking the best for her daughter-in-law, Naomi encourages Ruth to present herself to Boaz, who chooses to marry her. They have a son, Obed, who becomes the father of Jesse and the grandfather of David the king. In short, because of Ruth's friendship and love for Naomi, and Naomi's gratitude and love in return, God grafts Ruth into the lineage of Jesus.

The Bible's next book, 1 Samuel, speaks of the friendship of Ruth's great-grandson, David, with Jonathan, the son of King Saul. In chapters 18 to 20, 1 Samuel says that "the soul of Jonathan was knit to the soul of David, and Jonathan loved him as his own soul." It's fashionable in some quarters today to try to tease out a sexual relationship between David and Jonathan from the biblical material, but this simply confirms the insight of C. S. Lewis mentioned above. Nothing in the text suggests anything more than a deep fraternal loyalty between two close friends and fellow warriors: a fact of life in societies fighting for their survival. Saul is mercurial and intensely jealous of his throne. He repeatedly plots to kill David. And Jonathan repeatedly warns and defends David, finally triggering the rage of his father toward himself and forcing David to flee.

In the New Testament, Jesus calls his Apostles "friends," not servants (Jn 15:14–15). His friendship with Peter, the rock; John, the beloved; and James the Greater, who was John's elder brother, is especially close. All three, and only these three, witness the Lord's Transfiguration.

The friendship Christ has with each of his twelve Apostles is unique and personal, born from the "work" of his mission. With Martha, Mary, and Lazarus, the friendship Jesus shares is more one of affection, tenderness, and rest. When Jesus weeps at the news of Lazarus's death, his tears are for the loss of a friend, and they flow from deep and very human emotions.

Friendship suffuses the Acts of the Apostles and the epistles. The Church grew and thrived through friends sharing the joy they found in the Gospel. Paul's hugely fruitful missionary journeys depended on the support he drew from friendships with Barnabas, John Mark, Timothy, and others. The nature of Christian *philia* or friendship-love is expressed best perhaps in the Letter to the Colossians: "Put on then, as God's chosen ones, holy and beloved, compassion, kindness, lowliness, meekness, and patience, forbearing one another and, if one has a complaint against another, forgiving each other; as the Lord has forgiven you, so also you must forgive. And above all these, put on love, which binds everything together in perfect harmony" (3:12–14).

In the Gospel of John, Jesus tells us to "love one another as I have loved you," and "Greater love has no man than this, that a man lay down his life for his friends" (15:12–13). The crowning achievement of the Christian life is a community animated and ruled by *agape* (unselfish love) because of the free and generous *philia* (friendship-love) of its members. How do we get that? Jesus told us quite clearly. He left us the instructions on the night before he laid down his own life for all of us as his friends. And we hear his command in every Eucharistic Prayer in every sacrifice of the Mass:

Do this in memory of me.

ℒ

I BEGAN THIS book with some thoughts on the importance of memory. And early on, I quoted one of the poems that has always lived in my own memory. Dylan Thomas wrote "Do not go gentle into that good night," addressed to his father, in 1947. And the lines of that poem, even today, are incandescent: *Do not go gentle into that good night, / Old age should burn and rave at close of day; / Rage, rage, against the dying of the light.*

In a later stanza, Thomas speaks of good men *crying how bright / Their frail deeds might have danced in a green bay, / Rage, rage, against the dying of the light.*

As we age, unless we walk in a friendship with God and others who love him, memory can become as much a burden as a solace. It's easy to tangle our hearts in a web of nostalgia and old resentments; to nearly drown, like Bunyan's Pilgrim, in a river of past failures, sins, and "frail deeds [that] might have danced in a green bay." The mind can wander over a lot of accumulated terrain. We think, "If only I'd had more time, I could have accomplished" this or that. Or, "Why didn't I do X when I had the chance?" It's a long, self-examining litany; the same litany—in different ways, with different details—that presents itself near the end of every life.

My own generation, born on the seam of the "silent" and boomer generations, is now passing off the stage. It did many things beautiful and life-giving, and many others wicked and destructive. We humans can be very skilled at basking in the glow of the good we did, and the even greater good we intended. I needn't feed that habit here. Nor do I think my generation very different from or worse than many others that came before it. But tipping points in the life of a people, a culture, and a nation do happen; points beyond which everyday reality is changed in kind, not merely in degree. We're living such a moment today. And because we're within it, we won't understand its implications clearly until the future renders our time now in the rearview mirror, as a series of formative events in the past.

What the future holds is thus always ambiguous, and the temptation to fear can be strong. The United States—my home—remains a great and, in its best ideals, a *good* nation. But it's also a nation of chronic racial injustice, deep sexual dysfunctions, self-flattering elites, great disparities in wealth, and the intentional destruction of more than 50 million unborn children, entire generations of a now-dead future. These things carry a heavy social mortgage, a balloon payment that must and will come due.

Our internal divisions as a nation now run bitter and deep. For too many of us, freedom no longer means the ability to know, to choose, and to do what's morally right; rather, it means what the scholar D. C. Schindler described as "freedom from reality" itself. It's a freedom literally "diabolical" in the sense of the original Greek roots of the word: *dia* (between) and *ballo* (throw), meaning roughly to split apart or divide.[7] As a result, we relentlessly try to reimagine the world to suit our desires, and then coerce others into believing our delusions. We deconstruct human nature and sexual identity with spurious gender theory. And we produce cancerous judicial decisions like the June 2020 Supreme Court rulings in *Bostock v. Clayton County* and *Harris Funeral Homes v. Equal Employment Opportunity Commission*.[8]

Yet the Word of God, in *every* generation, again and again, reminds us to hope, and Scripture is the record and the proof of God's fidelity. So as Christians, how do we live and die with a spirit of truth in a "cancel culture" of growing deceit? How do we nourish joy and peace in our own lives, in those we love, and in those who look to us for example?

I've kept two of Henri de Lubac's quotations close to my heart for many years; I reread them often, and they're worth sharing here.

Here's the first: "*All [our religious] formulas, all the precautions of orthodoxy, all the scruples of literal conformity . . . are powerless to safeguard the purity of the faith. If the spirit should be lacking, dogma becomes no more than a myth and the Church no more than a party.*"[9] Lubac's words remind us that our faith as Catholics is finally about trust, not ideas or structures, as vital as those things often are. It's about a friendship with God that radiates outward to embrace and draw in others. It's about knowing, and loving, and following Jesus Christ as the friends he intended us to be—not merely "knowing about" him, but knowing *him*. Without a passion in our hearts for the living person of Jesus Christ, our faith is empty. *With* it, all things are possible.

Scripture tells us that love is strong as death and a seal upon the heart (Song 8:6). But we need to believe more zealously and go even further: *Love is stronger than death*. It's the seal that binds Christians together as a family across borders, hardships, persecutions, and time, across all generations of faith that came before and will follow after us. The Church is always weak, but her Lord is always strong. Empires and tyrants, ideologues and cynics, have learned that the hard way and gone down in the dust. The Church and the Word of God remain.

My second Lubac quotation, and the one I treasure even more, is this: "*I do not have to win the world, even for Christ: I have to save my soul. That is what I must always remember, against the temptation of success in the apostolate. And so I will guard myself against impure means. It is not our mission to make truth triumph, but to testify for it.*"[10] God will handle the rest. He's good at that.

We do have obligations in the world, duties that deny us the convenience of silence in the public square or escaping today's conflicts by hiding in the hills. As a bishop 1,600 years ago, Augustine stayed with his people, encouraging, inspiring, and comforting them, even with an enemy at the gates of his city and the Roman world falling apart. Likewise today, we need to do whatever we can, however modest and wherever life places us, to encourage our friends in Jesus Christ and to make the world a better place in the light of the Gospel. God asks nothing more of us, but also nothing less. And we're not alone. We're never alone. Nor, with fellow pilgrims on the road, are we ever "powerless."

I'll end with a story. A friend of mine was a student in France in 1967–68 at the Catholic University of the West. And one day her class visited a château in the Loire Valley. The docent took them into a room with an enormous stretch of hanging fabric, many yards across from one wall to the other. And on the fabric were hundreds of ugly knots and tangles of stray thread in a chaos of confused shapes that made very little sense. And the docent said, "This is what the artist saw as he worked."

Then she led my friend and her class around to the front of the fabric. And what they saw there is the great tapestry of the Apocalypse of St. John, the story of the book of Revelation in ninety immense panels. Created between 1377 and 1382, it's one of the most stunning and beautiful expressions of medieval civilization, and among the greatest artistic achievements of the European heritage.

The point is simply this: We rarely see the full effects of the good we do in this life. So much of what we do seems a tangle of frustrations and failures. We don't see—on this side of the tapestry—the pattern of meaning that our faith weaves. But one day we'll stand on the other side. And on that day, we'll see the beauty that God has allowed us to add to the great story of his creation, the richness we've added to the lives of our family and friends, the mark for the better we've left on the world, and the revelation of his love that goes from age to age no matter how good or bad the times. We are each an unrepeatable, infinitely treasured part of that story.

And this is why our lives matter.

NOTES

CHAPTER 1

1. "Quote 6," Israeli Ministry of Foreign Affairs, accessed August 1, 2020, https://mfa.gov.il/MFA/Quotes/Pages/Quote-6.aspx.
2. See, for example, Emine Saner, "What Is Jerusalem Syndrome?," *Guardian*, London, January 16, 2018.
3. Jonathan Riley-Smith's body of scholarship on the Crusades is extensive. Two of his books make for good initial reading: *The First Crusade and the Idea of Crusading* (Philadelphia: University of Pennsylvania Press, 1986) and *The First Crusaders: 1095–1131* (New York: Cambridge University Press, 1997).
4. Martin Mosebach, *The 21: A Journey into the Land of Coptic Martyrs* (Walden, NY: Plough Publishing, 2019).
5. All J. H. Plumb quotations are taken from his text *The Death of the Past* (New York: Palgrave Macmillan, 1969).
6. Philip Zaleski and Carol Zaleski, *The Fellowship: The Literary Lives of The Inklings* (New York: Farrar, Straus and Giroux, 2015), 188. See also Joseph Pearce, "J.R.R. Tolkien: Truth and Myth," *Lay Witness*, September 2001, https://www.catholiceducation.org/en/culture/art/j-r-r-tolkien-truth-and-myth.html.
7. Simone Weil, *Waiting for God* (New York: Harper Perennial, 2009); see the section "Read On," 15.

8. J. R. R. Tolkien, *The Two Towers* (New York: Houghton Mifflin, 1982), 697.

CHAPTER 2

1. C. S. Lewis, *The Screwtape Letters* (New York: Macmillan, 1982), 97.
2. Hilary Brueck, "Composting Human Bodies to Turn Them into Soil Will Soon Be Legal in One US State—Part of a Growing Green Death Trend," *Business Insider*, May 25, 2019, https://www.businessinsider.com/washington-state-human-compost-bodies-into-soil-2019-5.
3. Joseph Ratzinger, *Introduction to Christianity*, 2nd ed., trans. J. R. Foster (San Francisco: Ignatius Press, 2004), 72–73.
4. Hans Jonas, *Mortality and Morality: A Search for Good After Auschwitz*, ed. Lawrence Vogel (Evanston, IL: Northwestern University Press, 1996), 83ff.
5. Jonas, *Mortality and Morality*, 87–90.
6. Thomas Aquinas, for example, argues that it is unreasonable to think that animals would not have killed one another, since "the nature of animals was not changed by man's sin" (*Summa Theologiae* I, q. 96, a. 1 ad 2).
7. Aquinas, *Summa Theologiae* I-II, q. 82, a. 3; q. 85, a. 5.
8. This description of death in the Old Testament, and the location of many passages pertaining to death in both Testaments, are indebted to Alice Ogden Bellis, "Death," in *Eerdmans Dictionary of the Bible*, ed. David Noel Freedman (Grand Rapids, MI: Wm. B. Eerdmans Publishing Co., 2000), 330–31.
9. See Choon-Leong Seow's introduction to Ecclesiastes in *The New Oxford Annotated Bible*, 4th ed., ed. Michael D. Coogan (New York: Oxford University Press, 2010), 935–36.
10. Kevin J. Madigan and Jon D. Levenson, *Resurrection: The Power of God for Christians and Jews* (New Haven, CT: Yale University Press, 2008), 73.
11. Madigan and Levenson, *Resurrection*, 79–80.
12. Madigan and Levenson, 47.
13. Joseph Ratzinger, Pope Benedict XVI, *Jesus of Nazareth: Part Two: Holy Week: From the Entrance into Jerusalem to the Resurrection*,

trans. Vatican Secretariat of State (San Francisco: Ignatius Press, 2011), 155.

14. Ratzinger (Benedict XVI), *Jesus of Nazareth*, 244.

15. Gerard Manley Hopkins, *Gerard Manley Hopkins: The Major Works* (New York: Oxford University Press, 2002), 295.

16. Cicero, *Tusculan Disputations*, trans. J. E. King (Cambridge, MA: Harvard University Press, 1971), I.VIII.16.

17. Cicero, *Tucsulan Disputations*, I.XLIX.117–18.

18. It's also not a thing of the past. Especially in Silicon Valley, the Stoics are making a comeback. For example, see Olivia Goldhill, "Silicon Valley Tech Workers Are Using an Ancient Philosophy Designed for Greek Slaves as a Life Hack," *Quartz*, December 17, 2016, https://qz.com/866030/stoicism-silicon-valley-tech-workers -are-reading-ryan-holiday-to-use-an-ancient-philosophy-as-a-life -hack/.

19. Nicholas Diat, *A Time to Die: Monks on the Threshold of Eternal Life*, trans. Mary Dudro (San Francisco: Ignatius Press, 2019), 71.

20. Diat, *A Time to Die*, 13.

21. Diat, 30–31.

22. Diat, 28.

23. Diat, 93.

24. Diat, 114.

25. Diat, 161.

26. Diat, 78.

27. Richard John Neuhaus, "On Loving the Law of God," *First Things*, February 2009, accessed January 17, 2020, https://www.firstthings .com/article/2009/02/on-loving-the-law-of-god.

CHAPTER 3

1. Daniel Henninger, "America's New Nihilism," *Wall Street Journal*, June 4, 2020.

2. Susan Stamberg, "After 75 Years, Here's Looking at You, 'Casablanca,'" NPR, February 24, 2017, https://www.npr.org/2017/02 /24/515372794/after-75-years-heres-looking-at-you-casablanca. See also Aljean Harmetz, *The Making of Casablanca: Bogart, Bergman, and World War II* (New York: Hyperion, 2002).

3. Roger Scruton, "Forgiveness and Irony: What Makes the West Strong," *City Journal*, Winter 2009, https://www.city-journal.org /html/forgiveness-and-irony-13144.html.

4. Scruton, "Forgiveness and Irony." See also "Defending the West" in Scruton's *Confessions of a Heretic: Selected Essays* (London: Notting Hill Editions, 2017), 172–94.

5. Scruton, "Forgiveness and Irony."

6. Brad S. Gregory, "Science Versus Religion? The Insights and Over-sights of the 'New Atheists,'" *Logos* 12, no. 4 (September 2009): 17–55.

7. Yoram Hazony, "The Dark Side of the Enlightenment," *Wall Street Journal*, April 7–8, 2018.

8. Hazony, "The Dark Side of the Enlightenment."

9. Jo Craven McGinty, "The Young Are Having Less Sex, More STDs," *Wall Street Journal*, October 19–20, 2019.

10. Byung-Chul Han, *The Agony of Eros*, trans. Erik Butler (Cambridge, MA: MIT Press, 2017), 32.

11. Janet Adamy, "U.S. Marriage Rate Plunges to Lowest Rate on Record," *Wall Street Journal*, April 30, 2020.

12. Liza Lin and Josh Chin, "U.S. Companies Prop Up China's Surveil-lance Network," *Wall Street Journal*, November 27, 2019.

13. Austen Hufford, "Factories Seek White-Collar Degrees for Blue-Collar Work," *Wall Street Journal*, December 10, 2019.

14. Roger Kimball, "Civilization Is History at Yale," *Wall Street Journal*, January 29, 2020.

15. Wendell Berry, *Sex, Economy, Freedom & Community: Eight Essays* (Berkeley, CA: Counterpoint, 2018), 23.

16. Yuval Levin, *The Tyranny of Reason: The Origins and Consequences of the Social Scientific Outlook* (Lanham, MD: University Press of America, 2001), xxii.

17. Herbert McCabe, OP, *The Good Life: Ethics and the Pursuit of Happiness* (New York: Continuum, 2005), 10.

18. Roger Scruton, *The Face of God: The Gifford Lectures* (New York: Bloomsbury Publishing, 2012), 129.

19. Scruton, *The Face of God*, 72.

20. Centers for Disease Control and Prevention, "Suicide Rates Rising Across the U.S.," press release, *Vital Signs*, June 7, 2018, https://www .cdc.gov/media/releases/2018/p0607-suicide-prevention.html.

21. Tori Marsh, "Depression and Anxiety Prescriptions Are Climbing Nationwide," GoodRx, May 2, 2019, https://www.goodrx.com/blog/depression-and-anxiety-prescriptions-are-climbing-nationwide/.

CHAPTER 4

1. To paraphrase the French mathematician Pierre-Simon, marquis de Laplace.
2. Scott Hahn, *A Father Who Keeps His Promises: God's Covenant Love in Scripture* (Cincinnati: Servant, 1998).
3. See notes from Adele Berlin and Marc Zvi Brettler, eds., *The Jewish Study Bible* (New York: Oxford University Press, 2004), 110.
4. Ursula K. Le Guin's fantasy classic *A Wizard of Earthsea* is based on this idea.
5. Rémi Brague, *On the God of the Christians (and on one or two others)*, trans. Paul Seaton (South Bend, IN: St. Augustine's Press, 2013), 32.
6. Joseph Ratzinger, *On the Way to Jesus Christ*, trans. Michael J. Miller (San Francisco: Ignatius Press, 2005), 18–19.
7. Ratzinger, *On the Way*, 22.
8. Ratzinger, 26–27.
9. Susan Ackerman, "Idol, Idolatry," in *Eerdmans Dictionary of the Bible*, ed. David Noel Freedman (Grand Rapids, MI: Wm. B. Eerdmans Publishing Co., 2000), 626.
10. Brague, *On the God*, 135.
11. R. R. Reno, "Pride and Idolatry," *Interpretation* 60, no. 2 (April 2006): 168.
12. Reno, "Pride and Idolatry," 176.
13. Reno, 176.
14. Rémi Brague, *The Kingdom of Man: Genesis and Failure of the Modern Project*, trans. Paul Seaton (Notre Dame, IN: University of Notre Dame Press, 2018), 21.
15. For more on Renaissance humanism, see James Hankins, *Virtue Politics: Soulcraft and Statecraft in Renaissance Italy* (Cambridge, MA: Harvard University Press, 2019).
16. Brague, *Kingdom of Man*, 185.

17. Brague, 160.
18. Brague, 202.
19. Brague, 205.
20. Brague, 214.
21. Jacques Barzun, *From Dawn to Decadence: 1500 to the Present: 500 Years of Western Cultural Life* (New York: HarperCollins, 2000), xvi.
22. Ross Douthat, *The Decadent Society: How We Became the Victims of Our Own Success* (New York: Avid Reader Press, 2020), 9.
23. Ratzinger, *On the Way*, 16.
24. Ratzinger, 29.
25. Brague, *Kingdom of Man*, 28.
26. Erasmo Leiva-Merikakis, *Fire of Mercy, Heart of the Word: Meditations on the Gospel According to Saint Matthew*, vol. 1 (San Francisco: Ignatius Press, 1996), 609.
27. Joseph Ratzinger, *Dogma and Preaching: Applying Christian Doctrine to Daily Life*, trans. Michael J. Miller and Matthew J. O'Connell (San Francisco: Ignatius Press, 2011), 299–300.

CHAPTER 5

1. Anonymous, *The Song of Roland*, trans. Dorothy L. Sayers (New York: Penguin Classics, 1957).
2. J. Glenn Gray, *The Warriors: Reflections on Men in Battle* (Lincoln: University of Nebraska Press, 1998). All Glenn quotations are taken from this text.
3. George Parkin Grant, *Technology and Empire* (Toronto: House of Anansi Press, 1969), 17.
4. Alasdair MacIntyre, "Is Patriotism a Virtue?," Lindley Lecture, delivered at the University of Kansas, Lawrence, KS, 1984.
5. Alasdair MacIntyre, "A Partial Response to My Critics," in *After MacIntyre: Critical Perspectives on the Work of Alasdair MacIntyre*, ed. John Horton and Susan Mendus (Notre Dame, IN: University of Notre Dame Press, 1994), 303.
6. Tom Holland, *Rubicon: The Last Years of the Roman Republic* (New York: Random House, 2004), xviii.

7. John Paul II, *Memory and Identity: Conversations at the Dawn of a Millennium* (New York: Rizzoli, 2005), see chapter titled "Thinking 'My Country' (Native Land—Nation—State)," 57–87.

CHAPTER 6

1. Yevgeny Zamyatin, *We*, trans. and int. Natasha Shell (New York: Random House, 2006).
2. John Courtney Murray, SJ, "The Church and Totalitarian Democracy," *Theological Studies*, December 1, 1952, https://www.library.georgetown.edu/woodstock/murray/1952a. All Murray quotations in this chapter are from this text.
3. Hannah Arendt, *On Revolution* (New York: Penguin, 1963), 49.
4. Niall Ferguson, *The War of the World: Twentieth-Century Conflict and the Descent of the West* (New York: Penguin Press, 2006), 397.
5. See Michael Burleigh and Wolfgang Wippermann, *The Racial State: Germany 1933–1945* (New York: Cambridge University Press, 1991). Also note Burleigh's *Death and Deliverance: 'Euthanasia' in Germany, 1900–1945* (New York: Cambridge University Press, 1994).
6. See Timothy Snyder, *Bloodlands: Europe Between Hitler and Stalin* (New York: Basic Books, 2010).
7. Quoted in Michael O'Donnell, "An Enduring Vision of Tyranny," *Wall Street Journal*, October 19-20, 2019.
8. The chapter source material here is well worth a reader's closer attention: Paul Johnson, *Intellectuals* (New York: HarperPerennial, 1990); Eric Voegelin, *Science, Politics & Gnosticism: Two Essays* (Wilmington, DE: Intercollegiate Studies Institute, 2005); James Billington, *Fire in the Minds of Men: Origins of the Revolutionary Faith* (New York: Basic Books, 1980); Michael Burleigh, *Earthly Powers: The Clash of Religion and Politics in Europe, from the French Revolution to the Great War* (New York: HarperPerennial, 2007); and Henri de Lubac, *The Drama of Atheist Humanism* (San Francisco: Ignatius Press, 1995). Eric Voegelin, who left Nazi Germany before the war, mentions the special importance of the Lubac book in his own text.

9. Alexis de Tocqueville, *The Old Regime and the Revolution, Volume I: The Complete Text*, ed. François Furet and Françoise Mélonio, trans. Alan S. Kahan (Chicago: University of Chicago Press, 1998), 85–86.

10. Tocqueville, 100–101.

11. François Ponchaud, *Cambodia: Year Zero* (New York: Holt, Reinhart and Winston, 1978), 192.

12. Yuval Noah Harari, *Homo Deus: A Brief History of Tomorrow* (New York: HarperCollins, 2017), 309.

13. Harari, *Homo Deus*, 343.

14. Nellie Bowles, "Tech C.E.O.s Are in Love with Their Principal Doomsayer," *New York Times*, November 9, 2018.

15. Jean-Marie Lustiger, "Modern Abstraction Is the Prerequisite on which Today's Civilization Is Based," comments to the International Conference on the New Technologies and the Human Person: Communicating the Faith in the New Millennium, cosponsored by the Archdiocese of Denver and the Pontifical Council for Social Communications, March 27, 1998. Private archive of the author.

16. International Theological Commission, *Memory and Reconciliation: The Church and the Faults of the Past*, December 1999, http://www.vatican.va/roman_curia/congregations/cfaith/cti_documents/rc_con_cfaith_doc_20000307_memory-reconc-itc_en.html.

17. John Paul II, homily, "Day of Pardon," March 12, 2000, http://www.vatican.va/content/john-paul-ii/en/homilies/2000/documents/hf_jp-ii_hom_20000312_pardon.html. Emphasis in original.

CHAPTER 7

1. Aristotle, *Ethica Eudemia*, 1242a40-b1.

2. The work of W. Brad Wilcox and the Institute for Family Studies (ifstudies.org) is one of several gateways to good data on the subject. See also Charles Murray, *Coming Apart: The State of White America, 1960–2010* (New York: Crown Forum, 2012); and James R. Stoner Jr., and Harold James, eds., *The Thriving Society: On the Social Conditions of Human Flourishing* (Princeton, NJ: Witherspoon Institute, 2015).

3. Erica Komisar, "'Mommy, I Like Coronavirus,'" *Wall Street Journal*, March 20, 2020, emphasis added.

4. Elizabeth Seay, "The Joy of Having the Family Together," *Wall Street Journal*, April 10, 2020.

5. Parmy Olson, "My Girlfriend Is a Chatbot," *Wall Street Journal*, April 11–12, 2020.

6. Allen C. Guelzo, "Rationing Care Is a Surrender to Death," *Wall Street Journal*, March 27, 2020.

7. Lauren Weber, "Mental-Health Requests Strain Employers," *Wall Street Journal*, February 13, 2020.

8. Andrea Petersen, "Are You Lonely? You're Not Alone," *Wall Street Journal*, March 3, 2020.

9. Clare Ansberry, "A Parent Talk, Before It's Too Late," *Wall Street Journal*, March 2, 2020.

10. Janet Adamy and Paul Overberg, "Marriage Is Becoming More Like a Luxury Good in U.S.," *Wall Street Journal*, March 9, 2020.

11. Adamy and Overberg, "Marriage Is Becoming."

12. Gina Tomaine, "I Kid You Not: Why Doesn't Anyone in My Generation Want to Be a Parent?," *Philadelphia*, February 2020.

13. See Mary Eberstadt, *How the West Really Lost God: A New Theory of Secularization* (West Conshohocken, PA: Templeton Press, 2013).

14. Robert Kraynak, *Christian Faith and Modern Democracy: God and Politics in the Fallen World* (Notre Dame, IN: University of Notre Dame Press, 2011), 215.

15. While a notion like "equality before the law" flows naturally from Christian belief, equality of outcomes, especially when pursued through command economies and political coercion, does not. The tyrannical potential of democracies concerned Tocqueville deeply. See Patrick Deneen, *Democratic Faith* (Princeton, NJ: Princeton University Press, 2005) and *Why Liberalism Failed* (New Haven, CT: Yale University Press, 2018). See also Ryszard Legutko, *The Demon in Democracy: Totalitarian Temptations in Free Societies* (New York: Encounter Books, 2016).

16. Michael Bordo and Harold James, "Economic Sustainability," in *The Thriving Society: On the Social Conditions of Human Flourishing*, ed. James Stoner Jr. and Harold James (Princeton, NJ: Witherspoon Institute, 2015), 132.

17. Yuka Hayashi, "Credit-Card Debt in the U.S. Rises to Record $930 Billion," *Wall Street Journal*, February 12, 2020.

18. David Harrison, "Shutdown Pushes Poorest to the Brink," *Wall Street Journal,* April 16, 2020.
19. Wendell Berry, *Sex, Economy, Freedom & Community: Eight Essays* (Berkeley, CA: Counterpoint, 2018), 151.
20. Betsy Morris, "Fortnite's Front Line," *Wall Street Journal,* December 22–23, 2018.
21. Naomi Schaefer Riley, "Preserving Real-Life Childhood," *New Atlantis,* Spring 2019.
22. See, for example, Julia Carpenter, "The Economics of Egg Freezing," *Wall Street Journal,* February 18, 2020; and Julie Jargon, "Apps Help Strangers Have a Baby Together," *Wall Street Journal,* January 8, 2020.
23. Brendan Foht, "The New Kinship Engineering," *New Atlantis,* Summer 2019. See also Christopher O. Tollefsen, "Making Children, Unmaking Families," *Public Discourse,* August 19, 2020, https://www.thepublicdiscourse.com/2020/08/70265/; and Matthew Lee Anderson, "Poly Parenting and the Value of the Family," *Public Discourse,* August 20, 2020, https://www.thepublicdiscourse.com/2020/08/70313/.
24. Gautam Naik, "Unwanted Memories Erased in Experiment," *Wall Street Journal,* December 23, 2013. See also Fiona MacDonald, "Scientists Already Know How to 'Erase' Your Painful Memories . . . and Add New Ones," ScienceAlert, February 15, 2016, https://www.sciencealert.com/scientists-have-figured-out-how-to-erase-your-painful-memories.
25. Shulamith Firestone, *The Dialectic of Sex: The Case for Feminist Revolution* (New York: Farrar, Straus, and Giroux, 1970), 11.
26. Wilhelm Reich, *The Sexual Revolution: Toward a Self-Regulating Character Structure,* trans. Therese Pol (New York: Macmillan, 2013).
27. See also the author's previous discussion of Reich and related issues in *Strangers in a Strange Land: Living the Catholic Faith in a Post-Christian World* (New York: Henry Holt, 2017), 82–104.
28. For an example of the not-so-implicit hostility in today's emerging "family science" to traditional family structure and its allegedly unjust "privileged" status, see Meredith Landry, "What Is Family Privilege: A Q&A with Professor Bethany Letiecq," *FamilyStory,* August 23,

2019, https://familystoryproject.org/what-is-family-privilege-a-qa -with-professor-bethany-letiecq/?hilite=%27letiecq%27.

29. Christopher Lasch, *Haven in a Heartless World: The Family Besieged* (New York: W. W. Norton, 1979), 96, 100, 174.

30. Christopher Lasch, *The Minimal Self: Psychic Survival in Troubled Times* (New York: W. W. Norton, 1984).

31. See David Redmon, "Playful Deviance as an Urban Leisure Activity: Secret Selves, Self-Validation, and Entertaining Performances," *Deviant Behavior: An Interdisciplinary Journal* 24, no. 1 (2003): 27–51. Public, transgressive sex during Mardi Gras is the example Redmon uses. But popular slogans like "what happens in Vegas stays in Vegas" imply the prevalence of similar, normally proscribed behaviors.

32. John Paul II, *Letter to Families*, Vatican City, 1994, http://www .vatican.va/content/john-paul-ii/en/letters/1994/documents/hf_jp -ii_let_02021994_families.html. All John Paul quotations in this chapter derive from this document.

33. Romano Guardini, *Learning the Virtues That Lead You to God*, trans. Stella Lange (Manchester, NH: Sophia Institute Press, 1998), 176.

CHAPTER 8

1. All papal and conciliar documents mentioned in this chapter are available online at www.vatican.va.

2. Joseph P. Tierney, "How Catholic Places Serve Civic Purposes: The Archdiocese of Philadelphia's Economic 'Halo Effects,'" Program for Research on Religion and Urban Civil Society, University of Pennsylvania, Philadelphia, PA, 2016.

3. Patrick Deneen, "The Rise and Radicalization of 'The New Class,'" remarks to the "The New Class and The Church" symposium, Archdiocese of Philadelphia, March 29, 2019.

4. Ian Lovett, "Religion Is on the Decline as More Adults Check 'None,'" *Wall Street Journal*, October 17, 2019.

5. Vincent Nichols, *St. John Fisher: Bishop and Theologian in Reformation and Controversy* (Stoke-on-Trent, UK: Alive Publishing, 2014), 93. Nichols, later cardinal archbishop of Westminster, drafted this excellent text as a thesis early in his priesthood. It was subsequently revised and updated.

6. Nichols, *St. John Fisher*, 91.

7. Noted by Roger Scruton in *The Uses of Pessimism: And the Danger of False Hope* (New York: Oxford University Press, 2010), 20.

CHAPTER 9

1. See Stephen R. Covey, *The 7 Habits of Highly Effective People: Powerful Lessons in Personal Change* (New York: Simon & Schuster, 2013).

2. David Goldhill, "There Is Someone Alive Today Who Will Live to Be 1,000 Years Old," *Independent*, London, May 8, 2018.

3. Leon Kass, *Leading a Worthy Life: Finding Meaning in Modern Times* (New York: Encounter Books, 2020). See the chapter "Ageless Bodies, Happy Souls: Biotechnology and the Pursuit of Happiness," 143–64.

4. Leon Kass, *Life, Liberty, and the Defense of Dignity: The Challenge for Bioethics* (San Francisco: Encounter Books, 2002). See the chapter "*L'Chaim* and Its Limits: Why Not Immortality?," 257–74.

5. Catholic teaching on the Last Things is beautifully outlined in Nos. 1020–1060 of the U.S. Catholic Conference's *Catechism of the Catholic Church*, 2nd ed. (Washington, DC: Libreria Editrice Vaticana, 1997).

6. Augustine, *City of God*, trans. Marcus Dods (New York: Modern Library, 1950), books XI–XXII, 345–867.

7. John Bunyan, *The Pilgrim's Progress* (New York: Barnes & Noble Classics, 2005), 173.

8. Bunyan, *Pilgrim's Progress*, 176.

9. Carl Trueman, "The Final Enemy," *First Things*, June/July 2020.

10. Joseph Ratzinger, *Introduction to Christianity*, trans. J. R. Foster (San Francisco: Ignatius Press, 1990), 249–51.

11. C. S. Lewis, *The Last Battle* (New York: HarperCollins, 2000), 175–76.

12. See the chapter "Secularizing Knowledge" in Brad S. Gregory, *The Unintended Reformation: How a Religious Revolution Secularized Society* (Cambridge, MA: Harvard University Press, 2012), 298–364. See also "Epilogue: Assessing the Reformations" in Carlos Eire, *Reformations: The Early Modern World, 1450–1650* (New Haven, CT: Yale University Press, 2016), 741–57.

13. Romano Guardini, *The Faith and Modern Man,* trans. Charlotte E. Forsyth (New York: Pantheon, 1952). See the chapter "Purgatory," 155–66.

14. Romano Guardini, *The Lord,* trans. Elinor Castendyk Briefs (Washington, DC: Regnery, 2009), 134. See also Guardini's discussion of "The Adversary" in *The Faith and Modern Man,* 139–54.

15. Joseph Ratzinger, *On the Way to Jesus Christ,* trans. Michael J. Miller (San Francisco: Ignatius Press, 2005), 91.

16. C. S. Lewis, *The Problem of Pain* (New York: Macmillan, 1962). See the chapter "Hell," 118–28.

17. Vladimir Solovyov, *War, Progress, and the End of History* (Hudson, NY: Lindisfarne Press, 1990), 165.

18. Roger Scruton, *Beauty: A Very Short Introduction* (New York: Oxford University Press, 2011), 145.

19. See the *Catechism of the Catholic Church,* No. 32.

AFTERWORD

1. Gilbert Meilaender, *Friendship: A Study in Theological Ethics* (Notre Dame, IN: University of Notre Dame Press, 1985), 1–2.

2. Meilaender, *Friendship,* 3.

3. Aristotle, *Nicomachean Ethics,* trans F. H. Peters (New York: Barnes & Noble, 2004), 160.

4. Aristotle, 203.

5. C. S. Lewis, *The Four Loves* (San Francisco: HarperOne, 2017); all Lewis quotations in this chapter are taken from his reflections on "Friendship," 73–115.

6. Kelly Grovier, "In the Name of the Father," *Observer,* London, April 28, 2007.

7. D. C. Schindler, *Freedom from Reality: The Diabolical Character of Modern Liberty* (Notre Dame, IN: University of Notre Dame Press, 2017), 7.

8. See R. R. Reno, "A Striking Display of Sophistry," *First Things,* June 16, 2020, https://www.firstthings.com/web-exclusives/2020/06/a-striking-display-of-sophistry; and Hadley Arkes, "A Morally Empty Jurisprudence," *First Things,* June 17, 2020, https://www.firstthings.com/web-exclusives/2020/06/a-morally-empty-jurisprudence.

See also Ryan T. Anderson, "The Supreme Court's Mistaken and Misguided Sex Discrimination Ruling," *Public Discourse*, June 16, 2020, https://www.thepublicdiscourse.com/2020/06/65024/.

9. Henri de Lubac, *Paradoxes of Faith,* trans. Paule Simon and Sadie Kreilkamp, and Ernest Beaumont (San Francisco: Ignatius Press, 1987), 20.

10. Lubac, *Paradoxes of Faith*, 72.

ACKNOWLEDGMENTS

I sat down to write these acknowledgments on the anniversary of my ordination as a bishop, one of the greatest blessings of my life. The years I spent in ministry with the clergy and people of Rapid City, and later Denver, are filled with wonderful memories. In fact, if I made a list of every good priest, deacon, religious, and layperson who has shown me kindness over the decades, or led me to be a better man through the tug of his or her personal witness, it would circle the globe several times. I owe a special debt to my Capuchin brothers and bishop friends, but all of these good people have made my life rich. Many of them know who they are. Others will find out when we (hopefully) meet in heaven. In the meantime, all are in my memory, my gratitude, and my prayers.

Philadelphia was my last assignment as a bishop, and in some ways the most demanding. I owe a huge debt of thanks to my brothers in the Philadelphia presbyterate and diaconate, to my senior staff, to the faculty and students of St. Charles Borromeo Seminary, and to the members of my Priests' Council and Archdiocesan Pastoral and Finance Councils. They were great sources of encouragement.

Bill Barry has been a colleague and friend, as well as my patient literary agent, for three different books. The original idea for *Things Worth Dying For* came from Bill's fertile mind, and I'm very grateful for his good humor, skill, excellent counsel, and extraordinary help over the years.

As C. S. Lewis once suggested, there is "[no] pleasure on earth as great as a circle of Christian friends by a good fire"—or at least sharing a good meal. In 2004, while I still served as archbishop of Denver, a small circle of men, both lay and ordained, came together every month in a Fellowship around my dinner table. Informal, candid, and fraternal, it has endured and deepened over the years, despite the distances and duties that often separate the members. Their support and friendship have been among the many great gifts of my life.

Thanks to Gerard Bradley, William Cavanaugh, Patrick Deneen, Brad S. Gregory, and Phillip Muñoz, wonderful scholars each, for sharing some of their time and thoughts as I started this project. Thanks also to Carl Trueman, David Scott, Helen Alvaré, Christopher Ruddy, and Alexandra DeSanctis for reading portions of the text and offering their comments; any surviving flaws in the material are my responsibility alone. Thanks to Donna

Huddell, Donald Antenen, and Jane Sloan Peters for their excellent research assistance. And thanks also to Suann Malone Maier for sharing her memorable story of the *Apocalypse Tapestry*.

I need to offer special thanks to my friends Nathaniel Peters and Rusty Reno. This book simply would not exist without their superior skill and kind help with certain key sections of the text. They, and other gifted Catholic men and women like them, are a source of hope for the Church as she faces a challenging future.

Last, but not least: Kerry Kober and Francis X. Maier each accompanied me in my ministry as a bishop for more than twenty years. I'm deeply grateful for their support in completing this book, and in so many other tasks over the decades. They were invaluable colleagues as staff. They were and are, in the truest Christian sense, also *friends*.

Philadelphia
July 26, 2020
Memorial of Saints Joachim and Anne

ABOUT THE AUTHOR

CHARLES J. CHAPUT, OFM Cap., was named archbishop of Philadelphia in 2011 by Pope Benedict XVI. As a member of the Prairie Band Potawatomi Nation, he was the second Native American to be ordained a bishop in the United States and is the first Native American archbishop. Chaput is the author of *Strangers in a Strange Land*, *Living the Catholic Faith*, and *Render unto Caesar*, as well as numerous articles and public talks. Having retired as archbishop of Philadelphia in early 2020, he continues his extensive writing and public speaking.